50 great curries of india
camellia panjabi

D1551524

Camellia Panjabi was born in Mumbai. She read Economics at Cambridge and went on to become the Marketing Director of India's most prestigious hotel group—Taj Hotels—known for spearheading new cuisines and culinary ideas in its Asian and Western restaurants. With a lifelong passion for food and for exploring different cuisines, Camellia Panjabi has helped create several restaurants for these premier hotels, featuring little-known regional dishes.

In 1982 Camellia opened the Bombay Brasserie in London, which introduced regional Indian cooking to the UK for the first time and changed the way Indian cuisine is perceived in London.

In 2001, she left the Taj Group to join her family's restaurant company, Masala World, in London, which owns Chutney Mary, Veeraswamy, Masala Zone, and Amaya.

50 great curries
of india

camellia panjabi

kyle books

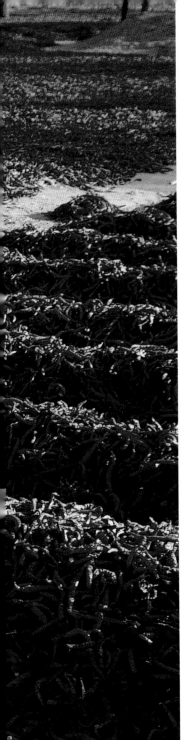

contents

This book is dedicated to the hope that the delicacy, depth and diversity of the cuisines of India may be better understood and appreciated in India and the rest of the world.

NOTE

Cooking times: It is hard to be precise about cooking times when preparing Indian food, as these depend to a great extent on size and cut of the pieces of meat, poultry, and fish, and on whether these ingredients are on or off the bone. It is important to check carefully that everything is cooked to your satisfaction.

introduction

Ever since I can remember I have loved and been passionately involved in food. From the age of five I wanted to be consulted at home on the menu that my mother discussed with the cook every evening for the following day. Lunch at school (Queen Mary's in Bombay, as it then was) arrived from home in a tiffin-carrier, as it did for everyone else, and a large, warehouse-like hall with four long rows of benches housed the 300-plus girls who mouthed their way through lovingly cooked meals from home, brought by *ayahs* and drivers. I often walked between the benches eyeing the plates, taking in the color, texture, and aroma of everyone's lunch, which always seemed more interesting than my own. Then in the evening I would explain to my mother in great detail what the dishes that I coveted looked like, and entreat her to make them for me. As I grew older I began to tell her the names of the recipients, hoping she would recognize the communities they belonged to, and hence the dishes that I was raving about. But knowledge of the cuisine of communities other than one's own was very limited in those days.

Strangely, it is only recently that I managed to track down the particular favorite (appearance-wise at least) of my childhood memories: a bright red curry that a Parsee girl sitting behind me often ate.

A few years later, due to domestic reasons, my sister Namita and I signed up for "school lunch", cooked and provided in a separate dining room for those children whose parents could not arrange for delivery of lunch to the school every midday. Our meal now consisted of "English food" (Queen Mary's was run by Scottish missionaries): baked fish, baked mince (cottage pie), *dhol* (an English and Anglo-Indian word for lentil dal) and yellow rice, mutton curry and rice, coconut pancakes, and Malabar sago pudding, the taste of which I had never encountered before. Later I searched for years for the exact replica of the mutton curry—once I found it accidentally on the buffet table of the old-world West End Hotel in Bangalore, only to return in the seventies to find that the cooks of the old brigade had retired, leaving no recipes.

When I went to university in England, I was astonished to find at college dinner that the dishes had none of the spices and seasonings that we had experienced in "English food" in India. It was then that I realized that "Indian English food" was a sort of hybrid-cuisine in its own right, and was fairly widespread, being popularly eaten in Indian clubs, where masala liver on toast was a favorite, on the railways which had to cater for British and Indian tastes alike, with the cooking done in cramped conditions by local cooks, and in *dak* government bungalows where masala omelet must have been and still is the number one seller. It was also eaten in popular restaurants like Gourdon and the Wayside Inn in Bombay, Koshy's in Bangalore and Flury's in Calcutta where cutlets were staple fare (though in Calcutta they are called chops). Incidentally, in India cutlets are patties made of a mash of anything—meat, fish, vegetables, or chicken.

As luck would have it, after a few years of marketing consumer goods in India, I landed in the hotel industry as the Sales Manager of the Taj Mahal Hotel in Bombay, a legendary hostelry about to embark on a once-in-a-lifetime renovation-cum-expansion program to double its size and add an array of restaurants and banqueting facilities. The hotel already had a fine restaurant which can be best described as "Indian French",

a grand ballroom where a buffet lunch was served daily, and a bar and grill. Next door was a sister hotel, the Greens, in the courtyard of which was an Indian restaurant known as Gulmohur, which served among other things the favorite Bombay dish, then newly discovered—Tandoori chicken!

In the mid-sixties my first mission was to increase the sales of this restaurant, where lunch-time business often consisted of six guests in an eighty-cover restaurant, with dinner for about twenty or thirty people who wanted only to sit in the courtyard and eat Tandoori chicken and naan bread.

Then, there was no more than a handful of Indian restaurants in town. It is indicative of the time, though, that when conceptualizing the new Indian restaurant for the Taj, the interior designer (a Swiss famed for his work on hotel interiors) decided he wanted to design the restaurant on the lines of a traditional south Indian temple with majestic carved pillars and a marble embellished dance-floor for classical south Indian dances to be performed every night. He wanted a grand brass oil-lamp to be placed at the entrance to the restaurant, for which the name suggested was "Tanjore", after the town in which the most beautiful temples of south India are located—and which has now been declared a world heritage site by UNESCO.

Some of us muttered that we did not know much about the food of the region and that anyway the food of Tanjore was more likely to be simple Brahmin vegetarian, and as such not to our guests' tastes. Believing that the food of the restaurant need not be related to the name or the ambience, the Tanjore lobby won, and the restaurant stands to this day. It was the turning point in the restaurant life of India, however, making it fashionable to go out and eat Indian food in an elegant atmosphere.

Over the ensuing years, I worked closely with a team of Taj colleagues opening hotels and new restaurants within the hotels in Madras, Goa, Delhi, Bangalore, Hyderabad, and elsewhere. Interestingly, attempts to introduce regional Indian dishes in various menus always met with consumer resistance, in the sense that customers continued to order mainly the Punjabi dishes on a menu. In India, the majority of those who eat out as part of their lifestyle are Punjabis from the state of 20 million people in the north-west of India.

They grow most of India's wheat and love their naans and paratha smothered in real ghee or butter, and their favourite dish is butter chicken—pieces of Tandoori chicken with tomato and butter sauce. Punjabis are the most outgoing of all Indians; they relocate themselves as corporate executives throughout the sub-continent, and when they go out they tend to eat their own food, wherever they are. Since they form the backbone of the clientele of almost every Indian restaurant in the country, restaurant owners are wary about directing the menu away from Punjabi favorites. Also, city-dwellers in India somehow feel that since they can make the local cuisine at home, why spend money on this in restaurants; when people eat out, their two favorite choices are Punjabi and Chinese!

This is the main reason why regional Indian food has not come of age, even in India itself. Restaurateurs are wary of setting up restaurants specializing in cuisines other than north Indian. Calcutta, for example, has no well-known Bengali restaurant, while the most popular restaurant in the city, Amber, serves Punjabi food to hundreds of customers every day.

It was to combat this despairing feeling that one would never be able to present regional Indian food other than Punjabi cuisine to a restaurant-going public in India that led me to believe that perhaps it would be possible to launch a regional Indian cuisine in England, where acceptance of Indian food is high and regional cuisines of all kinds were being launched. To test the water, I thought what better way to start than with the food of my own city? And so the idea for what was later to become The Bombay Brasserie was born, although the notion that Bombay had a cuisine that would interest the outside world seemed fanciful beyond words.

This disbelief was shared not only among colleagues but also by professionals in the UK. A leading PR agency refused to handle our account unless I agreed to drop the name "Bombay" from the restaurant name, saying their research showed the name was synonymous with squalor! There was immense pressure to do the usual thing—north Indian food, presented ethnic-style, with all the dishes served simultaneously in nice metal bowls, with part-silver service as would befit the launch of a Taj restaurant in the UK.

I spent a few months in London in 1981, visiting every Indian, Pakistani and Bangladeshi restaurant of repute, going to the markets, talking to a great many foodies, chefs of all cuisines, and restaurant owners, and built up a picture of different influences and consumer ideas about eating in restaurants at the time. Then I returned to Bombay to locate the kind of dishes that would fit in with what I had discovered. We took chefs out of the hotel routine and for several months worked at homestyle recipes from the communities of Bombay. And so the menu for The Bombay Brasserie evolved.

Everything else developed logically out of this. To eat a number of items simultaneously on a plate meant larger plates were needed, larger glasses, larger tables, and so on were required. We were finally able to bring to London a mixture of homestyle Bombay dishes such as fish with green chutney baked in a banana leaf, the streetside food, the *sev batata puri,* as well as the imperative north Indian favorites like Tandoori chicken, but extending the form of cooking to local ingredients like trout.

The Bombay Brasserie celebrated its tenth anniversary in December 1992, and over the years had given Indian cuisine a new perspective internationally. But even so, it was not followed by a string of successful regional Indian restaurants in the UK. Even in India there still remains only a handful, some of them specializing in north Indian cuisine. Perhaps a greater understanding of regional Indian cuisines will result in more regional restaurants. I hope my book plays its own part in this.

I often hear my non-Indian friends say that the best Indian food is to be had in people's homes. This is true. But Indian food at home is completely different from Indian food as most of the world knows it. In fact what most Indians know of food other than their own is restricted to what they eat in restaurants. Ninety-nine per cent of Indians do not have a tandoor and so neither Tandoori chicken nor naan is part of India's middle-class cuisine! This is so even in the Punjab, although some villages have communal tandoors where rotis (bread) can be baked. Ninety-five per cent of Indians don't know what a vindaloo, jhal farezi or, for that matter, a Madras curry is. This is Indian food as eaten in Indian restaurants outside India.

Indians coming from different regions, religions, and castes do, of course, share a common ethos with each other's cuisine in a limited way, a similar method of slow-cooking, and a commonality of food materials, particularly spices. They know their own cuisine well because, with the women of the house either doing or supervizing the cooking, traditions continue. But their knowledge of other cuisines is usually limited to those communities where they have friends and visit their homes for a meal. In any city in India there are several communities, including religions and caste communities. At weddings where guests run into hundreds, the cooking is done by special wedding caterers and each community has its own. And this sector is a repository of culinary secrets as much as in homes where cuisine is taken seriously.

In the quest for excellence in making well-known dishes, I began to look everywhere: an outstanding dish in a lowly eating house off a bazaar, a flavorful dish in an aristocrat's house in Madras, a crustacean curry at the table of Bombay's top society hostess, a great dish at the table of a gourmet family in Hyderabad, a third-generation wedding cook from Lucknow. Sometimes it meant piecing together different little secrets from several sources... and so a collection of recipes began to build up.

Then a couple of years ago, my sister Namita and some of her friends opened an Indian restaurant in London, called Chutney Mary. The menu was a very interesting one with a great many "new" dishes. Late one night she called me in Bombay. "Camellia," she said, "the world here wants magical curries. Do you have any in your collection?"

The word "magical" set me thinking. This was along the lines of the personal quest I had embarked on to discover what exactly made one version of a traditional Indian dish so much better than the same dish made by someone else who was also a knowledgeable cook. At the Taj we endeavoured to raise the standards of popular dishes to match the rising expectations of customers who wanted all the familiar dishes, but they expected the hotel restaurants to cook them so much better, and I was not able to pinpoint how to make that happen. My quest was leading me to the discovery that catering college-trained chefs were being taught by teachers of whom very few had accessed the real treasure storehouse of Indian cuisine. This storehouse was diversified among the professional cooks who had cooked for weddings and traditional banquets, the cooks who worked for families who took pride in their table, and quite a few housewives whose tables were legendary—those were all a class apart. And this was where gourmet Indian cuisine had been practised, apart from the older best hotels in each city which had in the early half of the century attracted the best Indian traditional cooks. These have mainly been replaced by a new generation of trained chefs from catering college, of whom a few having learned from the "magical" old hands in their kitchen soared above the rest. But by and large the limited recipes taught in the colleges were percolating down to all hotel restaurants, both in India and overseas. So I began to look for recipes which were better than the run of the mill. This book is the result.

Those who cook and those who appreciate good Indian food are today desirous of knowing more about traditional regional Indian dishes. And curries are the fulcrum of an Indian meal. A better appreciation and understanding of the differing tastes of the many regional cuisines of India will also enable hoteliers and restaurateurs to have the confidence to put such items on their menus. An awareness of the dishes will enable the customer and the chef to travel the same path together. And the fact that many men and women in India and around the world will be able to enjoy these dishes in their own homes has spurred me on to write this book.

I am indebted to all those who helped me: the many cooks, housewives, professional gourmets, those whose business it is to do party catering—all of those who shared their culinary secrets. It has not been possible for me to name all those who freely gave of their time and knowledge, but to them I owe a great deal.

The above introduction was first written in 1993 and slightly updated in 2002. A lot has happened in the world of Indian cuisine both in India and around the world since then. So a further update is called for.

North Indian food is still the most popular food of India, in terms of cooking in or eating out. In India we see now the beginnings of packaged Indian food, but sold in pouches rather than frozen or chilled. The interest in regional foods has grown and in the larger cities of India you can now find a few restaurants serving Goan, Keralan, Western coastal, and Chettinad (Southern Tamil Nadu) cuisine. However, the biggest explosion is in Chinese and Thai restaurants. Chinese cuisine has evolved into a unique blend of spicy Chinese combined with the Indian love of gravy—the best-selling dish across India at the moment is an invented concoction called "Chicken Manchurian"!

Two significant developments are the growth of vegetarian restaurants as well as the vegetarian sections of menus in most restaurants. And a penchant for cheese—there is almost an Indianized Mexican cuisine now, so I have included a potato curry with cheese in this edition.

The second development is the growing popularity of seafood in India. In Mumbai, which was always a seafood-centric city, many traditional south Indian vegetarian restaurants have been converted by the younger generations of the owners into seafood restaurants selling their own Manglorean-type cuisine—with quite some innovations—tandoori crab, lobsters, and shrimps with southern Indian spice marinades. Not everyone is *au fait* with cooking seafood at home, though more people would like to. Several new seafood dishes have been included in this edition.

The immense proliferation of Indian restaurants all over the world has led to an exodus of experienced restaurant cooks and chefs from India, including young chefs with just a couple of years' experience. The best Indian cooks are now to be found overseas! Even large cruise liners source cooks from India because of their multi-cuisine skills.

Catering colleges in India have now begun to teach the cooking of their own region and frequently hold food festivals of other regions. This has definitely helped in giving budding chefs a bird's eye view of different Indian cuisines. But when combined with the lure of going to work overseas very young, the serious groundwork, the maturing, and innovation in India of professional cooking is not taking place, as perhaps it should. It is interesting that while there are numerous catering colleges run by the government as well as privately owned ones, there is not a single serious culinary school in India.

In the UK, which has relaxed its immigration policy to facilitate the entry of specialized cooks, the standard of the general offering in Indian restaurants has improved tremendously in the last five years. So has the range of Indian foods in British supermarkets, an impressive achievement if you consider that no other international cuisine on supermarket shelves has such an emphasis on regionality of recipes.

However, these tastes are not as close to the taste of "real" curries that you can achieve by cooking with the right spices made to original recipes. So for curry aficionados there is a real pleasure in discovering that you can make dishes yourself that you would otherwise be able to taste only by going to a restaurant that has a cook from that region who takes no shortcuts. Or by visiting that region in India and have someone invite you home!

Okra (bhindi) *growing in a field*

culinary india

At different points in its history, India was influenced by many foreign cuisines as the result of invasions and rule by invaders. Another major influence on Indian cuisine, apart from these cultures in India, has been the ancient Hindu treatise on health, the *Ayurveda*, as well of course as the countless other traditions that an ancient civilization develops over the centuries. As Indians now relocate from one part of the country to another, and restaurateurs set up establishments in regions of India other than their own, cross-fertilization between the sub-cuisines of India is taking place. Enterprising Punjabi restaurant owners have taken Tandoori chicken, naan, butter chicken, *chole,* and *tarka dal* throughout India and abroad, and Punjabi cooking has begun to influence homestyle cooking all over India. The caterers of Udipi (a village near Mangalore) have given all India and many parts of the globe a taste of *idli, dosa,* and Madras coffee.

But many local Indian culinary practises are still little-known outside their regions. Political boundaries were drawn within the sub-continent after independence in 1947 and, today, although one may refer to the cuisine of a political state within India (based largely on language), the culinary boundaries do not necessarily coincide with the political ones.

As with all cuisines, the regional produce forms the base. The Malabar coast of Kerala, with its profusion of pepper and garam masala spices, uses these liberally in cooking, and most, though not all, Kerala food is spicy-hot. When it is not so, the restraining hand of Brahminism has come into play, as spicy food is said to activate sensuality and consequently inhibit clear and high thinking. So the food of the Namboodri Brahmins is mild.

Thus, the influence of religion and caste is also important. Within Hinduism there are two main streams: the Vaishnavites and Shaivaites—the followers of the gods Vishnu and Shiva. While the Brahmins in both communities are largely vegetarian, there is a larger incidence of vegetarianism among the Vaishnavites. Other religions, like Jainism, which was a reformation movement among some Hindus, advocate a strict code of vegetarianism.

Geography itself has a part to play. Along some coastal regions of India, notably Bengal and in Maharashtra among the Saraswat Brahmins, fish is eaten by Brahmins without losing caste. Climate, income levels, traditions, and beliefs all influence cuisine. So do the preferences of the palate which differ between communities. The food of the people of Nellore and Telangana (in Andhra), Chettinad (in Tamil Nadu), and the Syrian Christians (of Kerala) is fiery-hot. That of West Bengal is mild and sweet, while in East Bengal—now Bangladesh—it is much hotter, though the dishes in both Bengali cuisines are the same. The food of Gujarat is mildly spiced and sweetish—the people use jaggery in their cooking, even in savory dishes—while in nearby Rajasthan, with its arid landscape, the food is more pronouncedly spicy.

As far as curries are concerned, the rice-growing regions of India have a large number of curries with thinner gravies meant for eating with rice, while curries in the wheat belts of India have thicker gravies well-suited to eating with rotis and parathas. In this book an attempt has been made to give a glimpse of most, though not all, the cuisines of India, outlining their distinguishable differences. I hope you will be tempted to delve further.

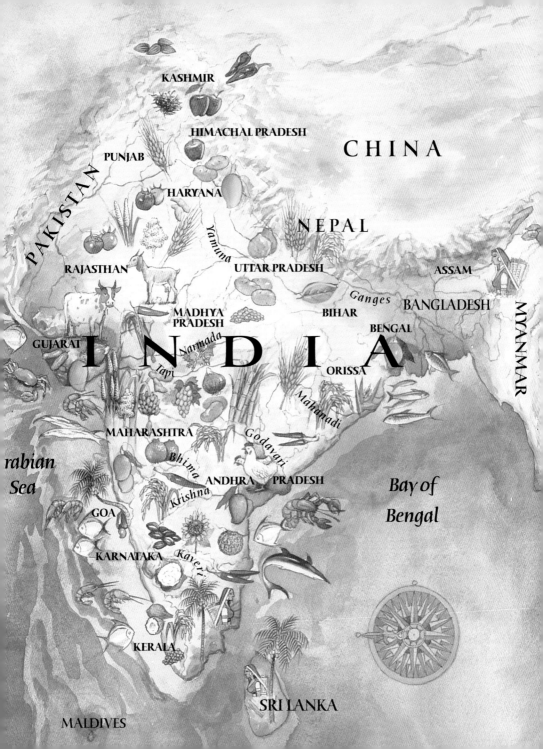

KASHMIR

HIMACHAL PRADESH

CHINA

PUNJAB

PAKISTAN

HARYANA

NEPAL

Yamuna

RAJASTHAN

UTTAR PRADESH

ASSAM

BANGLADESH

MYANMAR

GUJARAT

MADHYA
PRADESH

Ganges

BIHAR

I N D I A

Narmada

BENGAL

Tapi

ORISSA

Mahanadi

MAHARASHTRA

Godavari

Bhima

*Arabian
Sea*

ANDHRA   PRADESH

Krishna

Bay of
Bengal

GOA

KARNATAKA

Kaveri

KERALA

SRI LANKA

MALDIVES

the philosophy of indian cuisine

When I mentioned that I was writing an Indian cookbook to the famous chef and cookery writer Anton Mosimann, he said, "Do write about the philosophy of Indian cuisine. It's so difficult to cook something well without first understanding what the philosophy of the cuisine is." Of course, he is right. But trying to explain the philosophy of an ancient and complex cuisine in simple terms is no easy task, because one cannot describe the significance of one set of factors without outlining how it connects to others. So I will try to identify the various elements that underlie the system of beliefs on which the philosophy of Indian cuisine is based.

India is of course a sub-continent, equal in size to Western Europe, but without a single common language. It has about two and a half times the number of people, several language scripts and many more religions. So it is not easy to label its cuisine under a single heading. One has to allow for differences in climate and availability of produce, and vast differences in income among the people, as well as different religions, customs, traditions, and beliefs.

The strongest influence on Indian cuisine, or at least among 80 per cent of Indians—the Hindus—is Ayurveda, an ancient body of knowledge on health. *Ayur* is derived from the word *ayus* meaning span of life in Sanskrit, and *veda* means knowledge. Thus Ayurveda is the knowledge concerning the maintenance of long life. Its origins are in the *Atharvaveda*, the contents of which date from around 1000BC. Then in 200BC a medical treatise called *Charaka Samhita* was written in Sanskrit by a sage called Charaka, who re-edited *Agnivesa*, a text written earlier by a sage of the same name along with five others, outlining the science of prolonging life without illness. *Samhita* means compilation. It deals with the origin of medical science, a detailed classification of diseases, all food and drink substances and details of lines of treatment, the use of drugs, diet, and practices for achieving good health. In all, there are 150 chapters on specific topics.

Numerous other texts were composed through the centuries, and the Ayurvedic tradition continued as a vigorous and expanding scientific tradition up to the sixteenth century. Ayurvedic texts were translated into Greek by Cridos (300BC), Tibetan and Chinese (AD300), Persian (AD700), and Arabic (AD800).

Ayurveda is not confined to medicine only: it covers the whole subject of life in its various ramifications. It discusses the purpose of life, the importance of mental as well as physical health, and a code of ethical conduct for healthy living. The aim is salvation—to keep the body as well as possible and to give life such quality that one can progress beyond it. Life is a combination of the mind, body, and soul, and this is in fact the central subject of Ayurveda.

He alone can remain healthy, who regulates his diet, exercise and recreation, controls his sensual pleasures, who is generous, just, truthful and forgiving, and who gets along well with his relatives (i.e. enjoys a happy family life, in an extended sense). It is amazing that all these observations were made thousands of years ago, while it is only in recent times that scientists and thinkers have observed that a lot of diseases emanate from bottled-up emotions, grief, and negative thoughts.

Ayurveda understands the properties and actions of food differently from Western science. The bio-chemistry of an edible product is not everything. For example, vegetable oil and dairy fat, such as ghee from cow's milk, are not seen merely as fats, but also in terms of their effects on the body, which are supposedly very different. Ghee is cooling, while oil heats the body. Another special quality of ghee is that it assimilates the good properties of the foods it is mixed with and adds them to its own, without losing any of its own properties, while oil undergoes a transformation when it assimilates the properties of other food.

According to Ayurveda, the human body is composed of seven body elements or tissue layers. These are plasma (sometimes called the "skin"), blood, muscle, fat, bone, nerves and marrow, and reproductive secretions. And there are innumerable channels that supply the various tissue constituents. Good health means proper flow through these channels and an equilibrium in the proportions of the seven body elements.

Also, there are three primary life-forces in the body, or three biological humors. The Ayurvedic term for humor is *dosha*, that which causes things to decay. The humors correspond primarily to the elements of air, fire, and water, and in Sanskrit are called *vata, pitta,* and *kapha. Vata,* translated as wind, means that which moves—for example, breathing, and beating of the heart; *pitta* is fire, *dosha* translates as bile, that which digests things, including mental digestion, or the ability to comprehend reality; and *kapha* as phlegm, that which holds things together.

Ayurveda believes that when the humors are out of balance and aggravated, they manifest symptoms and give rise to various diseases. The excess humors move into the body's channels, causing improprieties in their flow. Diseases should first be treated with food, and medication only later if required. The treatments using foods are based on the six tastes (*rasa* in Sanskrit)—sweet, sour, salty, pungent, bitter, and astringent. Each taste has its specific therapeutic actions. The tastes increase or decrease the biological humors, as the case may be. Everyone needs a certain amount of each of the six tastes, and relative proportions differ according to the constitutional or humor type of the particular individual. Too much of any one taste is harmful to any constitutional type.

The sweet taste gives strength to the tissue elements, is good for nourishment, and harmonizes the mind. Sweet-tasting products are not only those which taste sugary, but include rice, ghee, and fruits. Sweet food is heavy on digestion, however.

The sour taste stimulates the digestive fire and enzymes and sour-tasting food, for example lime and tamarind, are easy on digestion and good for the heart. (It is only relatively recently that modern dietetics has decreed that vitamin C is good for the heart, and vitamin C is found in all sour foods!) By sour the Ayurveda means food that is naturally so, not man-made sour items such as vinegar.

The salty taste clears obstruction in the channels in the body, causes sweating, and increases the power of digestion, but tends to deplete reproductive secretions. An excess of salt causes greying and wrinkling.

Pungent tastes, as in onion, pepper, and garlic, help digestion, improve metabolism and dilate channels in the body. Foods with a bitter taste eliminate bacterial elements, purify the blood, and are light on digestion. Examples include bitter gourd, fenugreek seeds, and lemon rind. Substances that have a predominance of astringent taste, such as betelnut leaf, most green vegetables, and foods containing tannin like tea, possess the properties to heal ulcers and wounds. They dry up moisture and fat in the body and act as water-absorbents.

What I find most interesting is that the only other cuisines that give an important role to the sour, hot, and astringent tastes are those of Thailand and Indo-China, where through maritime connections Hindu influences have become assimilated. In fact, the ancient capital of Siam was called Ayuthya after Ayodhya, the capital of God-Hero Ram's kingdom in northern India, and the Angkor Wat temples in Cambodia have a Hindu influence. Galangal ginger (which has an astringent taste and features widely in Thai cuisine) is mentioned in ancient Ayurvedic texts as a medicinal plant.

A lack of any of the six tastes in the food will also aggravate the relevant humors. So now one can appreciate the *raison d'être* of the complexity of the Indian meal, which includes a spicy-sour taste mix, a yogurt-based item, a dash of a hot and bitter pickle (often lime with the bitter rind), and a sweet. The traditional Indian *thali* meal (served in several small bowls on a large silver tray) has been devised to contain these complex requirements in a way that can be replicated every day.

Ayurveda characterizes food and drugs in three ways:
1   By its tastes (called *kasa* in Sanskrit, which, as explained above, act on different humors.
2   By the potency (*veerya*) of the action it has on the body. All food items can be classified as either cold or hot.
3   By way of special action on the body (*prabhava*). For example, two food or drug items may be similar in relation to their taste and potency, but differ in their special action: for example, figs and dates are sweet and heating, but figs have purgative qualities.

Equally, all human beings can be classified into three mental types. A person is made up not only of physical or bio-chemical elements, but also of non-apparent constituents. These constituents decide the responses to stimuli that are received by the individual. These differences are governed by the qualities of *Satva*, *Rajas*, and *Tamas*. *Satva* means pure and therefore a person who has dominant Satvic traits will be a thinker on a higher

A typical everyday meal: dal and rice, potato with greens, yogurt, raw onion, lime pickle, and papad

plane, will have more curiosity, strive hard for real knowledge, and will try to win in competitive situations by adoption of fair means. A person who is Rajsic will be basically a doer, industrious and domineering, who will use almost any means to succeed. A Tamasic person will not even have a desire to learn or to put in effort and lacks the intellectual capacity to encompass the gravities of a situation.

Different types of food can contribute to a *Satva, Rajas,* or *Tamas* influence. Food that is easily digestible, fresh, and ripe, can be cooked by a simple and quick process (though not in a microwave oven!) and taken in moderate quantity contributes to the strengthening of Satvic forces. The person consuming such food is alert, quick-thinking, and in harmony with nature. He is stimulated by or quick to grasp even the slightest stimuli.

Highly spicy food, food produced by suppressive means (such as battery-produced eggs), or the meat of slaughtered animals is *Rajas*-dominant. The person who consumes such food loses the capacity to distinguish

the more subtle stimuli and as time goes on requires stronger ones to reach a good level of deep understanding.

Food that has a preponderance of oily and spicy ingredients and food that is overcooked, stale, and unclean, is liked by people in the state of *Tamas* or ignorance. All "junk" food would be included in this category, because it is prepared long before being eaten.

Ayurveda believes that sciences related to health and disease should make an attempt to study the omni-substances of behaviour, because the needs of personality types differ. The constitution of the mind has a role in preserving health and diseases of the body.

A practitioner of Ayurveda, when prescribing a diet for a person, would take into consideration his disposition, body type (which humor dominates his constitution), the season (because the humors behave differently in different seasons and food has to be adjusted for their heating and cooling properties), and particular state of health. He would tend to advise eating foods that grow in the region in that season. That is nature's way of balancing the requirements of the body.

The Ayurvedic texts also describe the methods of food preparation and consumption. Food should be prepared with love and good feeling. Hence even in affluent homes, in spite of having domestic help, many housewives cook for the family, though the help will prepare the food.

Food should be consumed in relative quietude, quite contrary to the Western emphasis on conviviality and conversation. Surprisingly, alcohol is not forbidden by Ayurveda. On the contrary, the *Charaka Samhita* lists eighty-four types of alcoholic preparation and claims that they strengthen the mind, body, and the power of digestion, and help in overcoming sleeplessness and grief. Practical observations indeed, and remarkably relevant today, considering when they were written!

Similarly, meat or fish is not expressly discouraged. In fact, the *Charaka Samhita* includes goat, chicken, antelope and turtle in those meats that are particularly good for health! However "we are what we eat" (*Upanishads*). Flesh has the force of violence in it, and the negative emotions of fear and hatred as part of it. It has therefore no place in a Satvic diet.

Generally, Ayurvedic teachings exhort people to follow a pure lifestyle, one that gives clarity and peace of mind. Physical purity involves a wholesome diet with emphasis on raw or freshly cooked vegetarian food, pure air and water, proper exercise of a calming nature (yoga), and physical cleanliness. Purity of mind involves non-violence, friendliness and compassion, and a means of earning a living that does not bring harm to others and provides a service to humanity.

why an indian meal?

The world's eating preferences are becoming unified. First, it was the high-protein diet that won a following, then the white meat variation of the protein-dominated diet took over. Now the world is moving towards the Mediterranean diet, dominated by carbohydrates and flavored with olive oil, tomatoes, and basil. Thai cuisine, with its aromatic blend of herbs, chile, ginger, and lemon flavors is becoming increasingly popular.

Indian cuisine combines all of these characteristics. It is first and foremost carbohydrate-dominated, with emphasis on wheat chapatis and rice as a staple food. Everything else is in a sense an accompaniment—curry, as we shall see, is a flavored dish to eat with Indian bread or rice. Unlike pasta, Indian roti is a wholewheat bread, retaining the entire goodness of the grain. Traditionally it was eaten with a dab of ghee, which is revered for its health-giving properties in India, but today uncooked oil is substituted. The rice that comes from the growing areas of the south is of the parboiled variety, partially boiled with the husk, then dried and milled, which retains more goodness than the polished variety.

Vegetables play a more dominant role in Indian cuisine than in perhaps any other. Usually one green and one other vegetable form part of every meal. India offers an array of vegetables unequalled anywhere in the world, and a variety of ways to cook each one.

Protein is also present in the Indian diet, of course, but much more effort is made to use protein derived from lentils and dairy products, rather than from meat. Legumes or dals boiled with herbs and tomatoes, seasoned with spices and eaten with rice, provide the amino-acid balance that constitutes "complete protein".

Meat and fish are eaten too, but in smaller quantities, well-spiced and flavored to give satisfaction. It is a little-known fact that even when affluent Indians eat meat, it is in a very small quantity per meal—about 4oz of meat, poultry, or fish on the bone. The composition of a meal would be about 2–3oz of actual flesh, a portion of vegetables, and maybe an additional root vegetable like potato, a pulse such as lentils, and a grain (wheat or rice), 2–3 tablespoons of raita (whisked and flavored yogurt), a little fresh herb chutney (for chlorophyl), and a cachumber of raw vegetables like onions and tomato.

The role of yogurt (which should be live) is very important because it introduces good flora into the digestive system. A vegetarian meal inclines toward being alkaline which is much better for health than an acidic one. But in India even a non-vegetarian meal is usually followed by fresh fruit which provides the alkaline balance.

As in Thai food, ginger, chile, and a sour accent are also essential, as are garlic and a range of spices. Spices play an important role in keeping the intestines decongested—they have an anti-inflammatory action, as in the case of turmeric; anti-bacterial, as with curry leaves; digestive functions, as with cumin and clove; and anti-flatulent properties, as with asafoetida. Certain spices have particular actions—for example, coriander seeds have diuretic properties and black pepper dries mucus. The composite effect of a combination of spices is to facilitate digestion and ensure a cleaner intestine, which is believed to be the key to good health.

In terms of use of time, Indian food has certain specific advantages. First, many items can be cooked a day in advance. The dough for bread can be made a day ahead, as can lamb, chicken, or fish curry which should be kept in a refrigerator: in fact, curries taste better the following day. Lentils (dal) can also be made a day ahead, but should be freshly seasoned. Vegetables are best prepared just before they are to be eaten, as is yogurt raita. Rice should also ideally be made fresh, though cooked rice can be eaten a day later.

What many Indian working women do nowadays is to make a fried onion, ginger, garlic, tomato, and spice masala mixture (daag) and keep it in the refrigerator for up to two weeks, or longer in the freezer. Whenever they want to make a curry they heat a few spoonfuls of it with some oil, add the meat, chicken, fish, or vegetables, and sauté for a few minutes, add some water and with no further effort they have a curry. Even when cooking a "dry" vegetable, they put a few spoons of the mixture in a wok, with maybe just $1/4$ cup of water, then add the vegetables and cook over a low heat. It is a simple and effective method, especially useful for working women.

Indian food is also quite economical to prepare as expensive cuts of meat are not essential, and, as explained above, you only need small quantities of meat combined with vegetables, lentils, yogurt, rice, and chapatis to make up a meal. With other additions such as chutneys, cachumbers, and papadams a table for an Indian meal looks quite bountiful.

To make a *daag* curry base for storing in a refrigerator or freezer:

2lb onions	4 teaspoons coriander powder
1 1/2 x 1/2-in piece of fresh ginger	1/2 teaspoon cumin powder
6 plump cloves garlic	1/2 teaspoon turmeric powder
3–4 green chiles	1/2 teaspoon garam masala
6 small tomatoes	1/2 cup chopped cilantro leaves (optional)
1/2 cup oil	1 teaspoon salt

1   Chop the onions finely. Chop the ginger, garlic, and chiles. Purée the tomatoes.

2   Heat the oil in a pan and fry the onions until dark brown (about 20–30 minutes). Add the ginger, garlic, and chiles and continue frying for 3 minutes. Add the coriander powder and sauté for 4–5 minutes, stirring continuously, adding 2 tablespoons of water if the mixture sticks to the bottom of the pan. Then add the cumin, turmeric, and garam masala. After 30 seconds, add the tomato and cilantro leaves. Stir, add 2 cups of water and 1 teaspoon of salt, and cook over a low heat for 15 minutes.

3   Remove from the heat, allow to cool completely, then store in a jar in the refrigerator or freezer. For 1–1 1/4lb lamb, chicken, fish, or vegetables, use one quarter of this mixture.

what exactly is a curry?

Curry, as the word is used today in India, simply means gravy. In the West, gravy is a liquid sauce made with juice from the meat, and thickened with flour and seasonings. Indian curry or gravy is made by cooking the meat or vegetables along with lots of ingredients including thickening agents and a combination of spices but using no flour. Western dishes most closely resembling curry are ragoût, navarin, and hotpot.

A lot has been written about the word curry and whether it was actually an Indian word in the first place, or invented by the English. The Tamils (the people living in the southern Indian state of which Madras is the capital) have the word *kaari* in their language, which has twelve vowels instead of the five in English and slightly different phonetic emphasis changes the meaning of a word. (*Kaari* is actually part of a longer word, *Kaikaari*, in the Tamil region, where caste differences are taken seriously, and these are reflected in different meanings of *kaari*.) The Brahmins of Tamil Nadu, who are strict vegetarians, mean by *kaari* a vegetable dish cooked with spices and a dash of coconut. When the non-vegetarian communities of Tamil Nadu use the word *kaari*, it literally means meat, which they pronounce with more emphasis on the end of the word as in *kaaree*. They would call a meat dish with gravy a *kaaree kolambu*, *kolambu* being gravy. **The origin of the word curry seems to be a meat or vegetable dish to be eaten with rice, which is considered to be the main dish of the meal.**

The English first established trading stations and factories (which in those days meant agencies) on the Cambay (west) coast of India in the early seventeenth century. But with Robert Clive's activities in Madras in the mid-eighteenth century, the English settlement there slowly grew into a thriving trading station, and much later women arrived from England and households were set up. Naturally, hiring of local cooks and servants followed. Hence certain regional dishes were borrowed and adapted—Tamil "pepper water" was one of these, with *muloga* (pepper) and *tani* (water) making up the popular mulligatawny soup. Even today the Anglo-Indians of South India make a soup called pepper water. Madras curry became synonymous with a hot curry: later on when people who were fond of curries returned to England, the curry powder trade was established in Madras where it continues to this day.

Cooks in English households in Madras would not have been Brahmins, who would have refused to handle non-vegetarian food. They would most probably have been from the castes who converted to Christianity, who would agree to cook meat. So they would certainly have referred to meat dishes to go with rice as curry.

In Northern India, particularly Punjab, *khadi* means a gravy dish made out of powdered gram lentil and yogurt which is often served with dumplings. Similarly, in Gujarati, the same word means a yogurt-based gravy eaten with rice. To the Sindhis curry means a lentil dish made with *thur* dal and gram flour, served topped with a medley of vegetables as a popular Sunday lunch dish, eaten with rice and fried potatoes. To the Bori Muslim community of Mumbai *kaari* is the Bori curry made with meat or chicken on a base of powdered peanuts and grams.

Curry means a dish with gravy, specially suited to combine with rice, and since it is widely believed that Indians always eat rice, does every meal include a curry?

In fact, rice is not always part of a meal except in Southern India and Bengal, and for the more affluent Gujaratis for whom rice follows the *poori* or chapati in a thali. The rest of India would have home-made roti made of millet or wheat, and only on some occasions would rice accompany roti, which would be eaten dipped in a dal or vegetable made not too dry as an alternative to a dish with gravy or curry. Similarly, rice is most commonly eaten with lentils, which would normally be accompanied by a vegetable. In affluent homes a dry meat or fish dish, such as a *bhuna*, might also be served with dal and rice, India's national dish, but this is not an everyday menu. The important point is that it is incorrect to think of rice and curry as inseparably linked.

A housewife choosing to include a curry when composing a menu, would do so in preference to a liquidy dal or a gravied yogurt (*dahi khadi*) to accompany rice and/or roti. The rest of the vegetables made would be dry. In such a situation she would make a semi-solid dal and would also choose to make a curry rather than a dry version of the meat so as to feed more people. Curry can be stretched even further if mutton or chicken, say, is combined with vegetables like potatoes, turnips, or spinach. The curry has to complement the other dishes served in terms of the quantity of gravy, color, flavor and spice. If other dishes are brown or yellow, a green curry such as meat with spinach would be suitable. And if the curry is going to be a brown one, it would go well with a yellow dal and a green vegetable.

In a way Indian cuisine is like classical Indian music. It has been handed down through generations without a written code. So curries, like other dishes, have always lent themselves to improvisation.

Since there are no rigid or classic recipes for any curry dish—any number of good cooks would have a different recipe for the same dish—one really has to search for the best-tasting version of a particular dish. This is, of course, how this book came about. Choosing a good recipe for a dish is a subjective matter, and means that you are free to change the recipe to suit your taste. You will not be breaking any rules in doing so. This is the interesting point about Indian cuisine. In addition to its immense diversity, it offers a great deal of flexibility. So please mix and match to suit your taste, and increase or decrease your ingredients as you prefer... just so long as you understand what each ingredient can do for you.

Let us now look at the basic principles of how to make a curry.

making a curry

The starting point in making a curry is to **choose a cooking pot with a non-reactive inner surface**. Most curries have a sour ingredient, so if a copper or brass pot were used it would have to have a tin lining. Stainless steel is better from the reactive point of view than aluminum or enamel but the pot should have a thick base or the spices will stick while frying. Traditionally in India, brass pots were used which were re-tinned regularly. In southern coastal India terracotta pots were and are still used, especially for making fish curries, as these have a strong sour tang. And as unglazed terracotta "breathes" and allows aeration, fish curry can be kept for a while without refrigeration in a hot climate. For fish you need a wide but not very deep pot so that the pieces of fish can be laid flat without overlapping. For a curry with lots of liquid a deeper pot is necessary. A flameproof casserole-type dish made of earthenware is ideal for making curries of all types, as are saucepans, particularly those with flared sides which make it easier to fry spices etc. Non-stick pots are suitable for Indian foods as onions and spices can be fried without sticking.

All curries have a main **ingredient** such as meat, fowl, eggs, or a single vegetable like potatoes, *brinjals* (eggplants), mushrooms, or a mixture of vegetables such as peas, diced carrots and french beans, or potatoes and cauliflower.

Most curries start with the heating of cooking fat. Traditionally Indians prefer to use ghee, which is clarified butter, believing it to be more nutritious and to give better flavor to the food. Ghee does indeed give a wonderful flavor but nowadays most people use oil instead because of the cholesterol factor. In western India, groundnut oil is most popular, in parts of south India it is sesame oil, while in Kashmir and Bengal mustard oil is used; sunflower and corn oil are also becoming popular throughout the country. You can use the oil of your choice. Because spices and onions have to be fried for a while at the start of making a curry, butter is not suitable as it burns and turns brown very quickly. The amount of oil needed varies with the shape of the pan. If there is too much oil, refrigerate the curry and the oil will solidify on the surface and can be skimmed off.

Ghee can be bought ready made. If you prefer, make it by melting unsalted butter and simmering it for 45–50 minutes until the solids brown. Strain through fine muslin or cheesecloth and refrigerate. The simmering time depends on the amount of water in the butter.

In Western dishes there are normally two or three main items in a sauce. Classic sauces are either butter and flour-based, or stock and cream may be used as a base, with the addition of wine. Apart from in the classic *bouquet garni*, or *fines herbes* mixture, herbs are often used in isolation.

Curry contrasts with this in many ways. **The base of the sauce, if non-vegetarian, is always stock.** Indians always use meat, chicken, or fish on the bone (we love to chew on the meaty bones while eating) to give the curry a robust flavor. The cuts include a few gelatinous pieces as well, to give body. For extra flavor, the shank bone containing the marrow is used.

Then there is always a second base or **thickening agent** to give the curry the required consistency: this may be onions, coconut milk, ground seeds or nuts—all contribute to the flavor, besides giving body to the curry. Flour is not used as a thickening agent as it lacks flavor.

The same ingredients may play dual roles or different roles in different curries depending on how they are used and combined to achieve texture or consistency, taste, color, and flavor. For example, onions, if puréed or lightly fried, may act as a thickening agent in one curry, while in another, if browned by frying, may give a deep brown color as well. Similarly, yogurt may give body to one curry, but work as a souring agent in another, especially if the recipe requires the yogurt to be a day old. So a curry recipe will be better understood if we work out the role that each ingredient plays in the recipe. The effect of each of the spices is a little complex. Spices are like musical notes. All melodies (or curries) are composed of the same musical notes (or spices).

1   **The choice of spices:** this makes the sum total of the taste and flavors.
2   **The sequence in which the spices are put into the pot** is important, as is the length of time each spice is fried and allowed to release its flavor.
3   **The ways the spices are used:** they may be fried or simply added to the boiling mixture. This is like the tone of the note—high or low. Frying releases the flavor of the spice more strongly than plain cooking.

The sequence of use of spices is important because each spice has its own pattern of releasing flavor with heat. With some this takes just a few seconds, others do better with being fried for a minute or more. If all the spices are added simultaneously, either some will burn or some will remain uncooked (or *kacha*), meaning that the flavor remains unreleased. Spices release their flavor in the most potent form in hot oil. Once moisture has been added to the mixture to which the spices are added, the release of their flavor diminishes. This includes the addition of ingredients like raw onions or tomatoes, as well as water or other liquid. For this reason onions are put in first, fried and their moisture reduced, before spices are added. So it is important to follow the recipes exactly, with the spices in the sequence mentioned, to get the flavors as they are meant to be.

For those who know a little about Indian cooking or enjoy Indian food, the importance of the word *bhuna* will be appreciated. It means frying either spices alone in oil, or meat or vegetables along with the spices, stirring continuously so that the spices are in constant contact with the hot oil and base of the pan, but do not stick. This process of **stir-frying**, which releases the flavor of the spices so effectively in the oil, is the heartbeat of a curry recipe. In some recipes spices may be put in at the next stage following the *bhuna* process, after water or ingredients containing moisture have been added. This will be done if the spices are meant to play a secondary note in the curry tune. This process also explains why Indian food in restaurants contains a lot of oil. If less oil is used in the *bhuna* process one has to stir constantly to avoid sticking, and this is labour-intensive. If enough oil is added to cover all the spices, three to four pots can be cooked at the same time, as the spices do not stick so easily. The second reason why restaurant chefs put a lot of oil into curry is that it helps the food to keep better without refrigeration if it is cooked in the morning to be served in the evening or the next day.

Many food writers and international chefs have mentioned to me that they find it mystifying how in Indian cuisine the same types of spices are common to almost every dish, unlike European food which has a different seasoning in each dish. Indian cuisine has a complexity of taste in its curry dishes, and a range of spices is used to create different tastes. It is the **relative proportion** of spices, the way they are used, as well as the **balance of spices with other flavorful ingredients**, that gives the final taste and flavor. For example, if a recipe contains a lot of red chile, but is combined with coconut milk, the red-hot flavor is balanced with sweetness, and when the proportion of coconut is higher than that of chile, the result is a delightful symphony of flavors.

Curries usually have one ingredient which imparts its particular characteristic **color** and another which gives a sour tang, an important element in the complexity of flavor when combined with other ingredients. But more of that later in this chapter. Another important point to note at this stage is the **strength of the heat**. Curry was traditionally cooked over firewood or coal. Even today, the very best Indian food made by traditional cooks for important occasions will be cooked in this way in large brass or copper pots. Initially, the fire is medium-hot at the *bhuna* stage, but once this is done, the curry should be simmered on a very low fire, with the lid on so that the aromas do not escape. Traditionally at the final stage a couple of live coals are put on top of the lid so that a gentle, steady heat comes from the top as well as the bottom of the pot.

thickening agents

Many ingredients can be used in this way, the most common being onions.

Onions

Onions are used finely or coarsely chopped, sliced or puréed. The proportion of onions to the main ingredient of the curry is important, because this will determine whether there is a sweet element in the taste as well as the thickness of the gravy. The finer the onions are cut, the less time they have to be fried or otherwise cooked in order to blend perfectly into the gravy. Onions are also puréed before frying, or sometimes cooked in their own moisture without oil to give a thicker gravy with lots of bulk. This technique is followed more in restaurants than at home, and is called "boiled onion paste" by chefs. The longer onions are fried, the browner they will get and the deeper the color of the curry will be. They may be deep-fried until deep brown and crispy, and then ground or blended, and added to the gravy. This gives a good flavor and consistency: see the Lucknow Lamb Shank Korma on page 78.

When the onions are fried only until light pink in color, they will impart a sweetish taste to the curry. Certain varieties of onion, like Spanish onions, are too sweet to be appropriate for curry-making. The most suitable from the taste point of view are the French and the small pink English.

At the time of frying the onions, ginger and garlic are often added too. Garlic browns quicker than onions, and so it is usually added later. The exact timing is specified in each recipe.

Yogurt

Yogurt (always known as curd in India) gives body and a creamy texture to a curry, but Indians mostly use yogurt as a "souring" agent (see page 38).

Cream (*malai*) and "hung" yogurt

In certain dishes, particularly in the Ganges plain; cream or *malai*, as it is called in Northern India, is used. It was incorporated into later Moghlai cooking under the influence of the local cuisine of the dairy-dominated region around Faizabad and Lucknow. Similarly yogurt is used in a concentrated form, after being left to hang in a muslin cloth, so that the whey drains away. In this way, the yogurt does not develop a grainy texture during cooking.

Coconut milk

Coconut flesh is ground to a paste with spices, or the flesh is grated and then soaked in water for 30 minutes, or blended to extract coconut milk. The first extract is thicker. The grated coconut may then be soaked in warm water to obtain a second extraction which is thinner. The second extraction can be boiled in the curry for longer than the first without releasing too much oil. When following the recipes, please do pay special attention to the details of how to use coconut milk.

Using canned cream of coconut, shredded coconut or coconut milk powder, or a bar of cream of coconut are other options. Frozen desiccated coconut often has a sweet flavor, depending on its origin, because in the West desiccated coconut is principally used in desserts. The flavor of fresh coconut is undoubtedly best, however. When buying a whole coconut, shake it to ensure that it has a little coconut water inside. This is a sign that the coconut is still fresh.

Using coconut
Coconut-based curries are *de rigueur* in the southern half of the Indian peninsula. Coconut is used in two basic ways. Either the coconut is ground (and sometimes grated and roasted before grinding) along with other spices, and the spice paste is then sautéed in oil. Or coconut milk is extracted by adding chopped or grated coconut to water, liquidizing it in a blender and then straining it. In this case the spices would be sautéed first, and the coconut milk added thereafter.

The taste of fresh coconut is not easy to replicate with processed products. It is unfortunate that supermarkets have not yet got round to selling freshly grated coconut (though frozen desiccated coconut is available— sometimes its taste is on the sweeter side) or freshly ground coconut, which would be so useful not only in Indian but also in Thai and Indonesian cooking. It is easy to extract coconut milk from freshly ground coconut too, by putting it into a blender with water, or just by soaking it.

I have tried dried desiccated coconut powder instead of both ground coconut and coconut milk, but it is not very effective. An exception is coconut powder, which is an acceptable substitute for coconut milk, although there is a variation in taste between various brands, some of which are better than others.

When using a fresh coconut, break it with a hammer or crack it open on a hard floor. Keep a bowl handy to catch the coconut water inside. There is a superstition in Southern India that a coconut should not be broken after sundown, around 7 p.m. But at all auspicious events, a coconut is broken on the ground—the equivalent of cutting a ribbon to open an event in the Western world. After the coconut is broken, the flesh needs to be carefully separated from the shell with a strong round-ended knife. Then the dark brown skin has to be peeled off as it will not grind properly. Grating is preferable, but grinding will take a shorter time. An effective grinder should be able to grind the coconut, even if you have to cut it into small pieces first, provided a little water (or, if the recipe demands, vinegar) is added.

A coconut-based curry cannot be stored for more than 8 hours outside a refrigerator without going rancid. In a refrigerator it keeps for up to 2 days. There is no problem in freezing such a curry.

pink onion

yogurt

half coconut

almonds

cashew nuts or other nuts

peanuts

white poppy seeds

gram flour

chaar magaz

white sesame seeds

roasted grams

lentils

Nuts and Seeds

Ground almonds, cashew nuts, and peanuts are sometimes used in curries, not only for their thickening quality but also for their flavor. Almonds were probably introduced into curries in India by the Moghuls and are widely used in the genuine Moghlai dishes, both of Delhi and the Ganges plain. In recent times almonds have become expensive in India, and since India is now a large-scale processor of raw cashew nuts imported from south-east Africa (Tanzania and Mozambique), cashews have begun to replace almonds fully or partially even in Moghlai dishes. In this book, there is a korma with pistachio nuts (page 110), which almost certainly has Moghul origin.

Peanuts, which are grown widely in Gujarat, are used extensively in the cuisines of the people of the region and around Mumbai, as a flavor enhancer and thickening agent in curries.

White poppy seeds are another favorite ingredient, primarily as a thickening agent in some Moghlai and Hyderabad dishes, and in the cuisines of the Muslim communities of Mumbai and Southern India.

Mustard seeds are used as a thickener to a lesser extent. Only in a few recipes are ground mustard seeds and methi (fenugreek) seeds used for this purpose. In Bengal ground mustard seeds are used widely, primarily for flavor, but they do also provide the curry with body since they are used in large quantities.

Pumpkin and melon seeds: another ingredient used in the court recipes of Delhi and the Ganges plain is called *chaar magaz*. *Chaar*, which means four, is a mixture of four kinds of seed—melon, pumpkin, squash, and watermelon. These are ground with a little water into a paste, and are again used both for the body and melange of flavors they give the curry.

Sesame seeds: *Til* are native to India. Ground white sesame seeds feature in Western and Southern Indian cuisine and the Muslim cooking of Mumbai, Hyderabad, and South India, giving a unique flavor to the food. The seeds are used in small quantities and therefore not as a thickening agent on their own, but with other ingredients. Sesame seeds are widely used for making sweet dishes. These are eaten more in the winter as they are believed to have heating qualities. In Maharashtra *ladoos* or sweet round balls of sesame and jaggery are distributed among friends and relatives on Makar Sankrant, the day the sun enters Capricorn—the beginning of the winter solstice.

Lentils

Lentils (dal) are either ground into flour or cooked separately and then puréed for use as a thickening agent. Dishes like the Parsee *dhansak*, the North Indian *dal gosht*, the Hyderabadi *dalcha*, the Bori Muslim *khichda*, and the Muslim *haleem*, are all examples of meat and dal dishes.

Recipes for *dhansak* and *dalcha* are given in this book (pages 114 and 98). The Sindhi Curry on page 166 is a vegetarian dal curry.

giving color to a curry

The ingredients that give color to a curry are:

1 Turmeric: **bright yellow**.
2 Saffron: **pale apricot**.
3 Red chiles: **reddish-brown**. The variety known as Kashmiri chile: **vermilion**.
4 Fresh cilantro leaves, if used in quantity: **green**. Darkens easily with longer cooking.
5 Red tomatoes: **pinkish** if combined with yogurt, and **reddish** if used on their own.
6 Onions: **deep brown** if used in quantity and fried until **dark brown** without adding much water.
7 Coriander powder: **deep brown** if fried for 5–6 minutes.
8 Garam masala powder: **deep brown** if fried for 1 minute.

If all these are used, then the ultimate color will depend on their proportions relative to the other ingredients used.

A field of onions in Kashmir

turmeric

saffron

kashmiri color

kashmiri chile

cilantro leaves

tomato

deep-fried onions

coriander powder

cockscomb flower

tandoori color

cockscomb water

cockscomb petals

souring agents

Since curry has a complex taste, and one of the constituent flavors is often a sour one, many curries contain a souring agent which, when used in conjunction with the hotness of chiles, and sweetness of onions, yogurt or coconut, gives a nice tang. Souring agents are more common among the curries of the Hindus. They are absent from Moghlai dishes, with the exception of those of the Muslims of Hyderabad which incorporate the sour taste—Hyderabadi food is a wonderful mixture of Moghlai and Deccani cuisine.

Tomato

Tomatoes were brought to India by the Portuguese in the sixteenth century but began to be widely cultivated for general use only in the twentieth century. Now they are grown throughout the country all the year round. Tomatoes have become a favorite ingredient in Indian cooking for color, flavor and the touch of sourness they give to food.

Even when ripe the Indian tomato is slightly sour in taste, compared to European or American varieties. Its acidity level is also much higher. When using tomatoes for curry-making, avoid sweeter Italian tomatoes.

Yogurt

Yogurt is always made at home in India, usually on a daily basis. Commercially made yogurt is a rarity. A little live culture is mixed into milk which has been warmed, then cooled, and left overnight. The tropical climate enables the yogurt to set easily.

Often, the Indian housewife will make a curry based on yogurt which inadvertently went sour. To sour yogurt specially for a particular dish, the procedure is as follows:

(a) use an already sour live culture to make the yogurt;
(b) use slightly more of the culture, say 2 tablespoons per 3 cups, instead of 1 tablespoon;
(c) mix the culture into the milk while the milk is still slightly warm;
(d) leave the yogurt to set in a relatively warm place. A thermos jar which has been slightly warmed by rinsing with warm water is suitable for making yogurt;
(e) use skim milk instead of full-fat milk.

When the yogurt begins to sour, drops of water will appear on the surface and increase as the yogurt becomes more sour. When it has reached the desired degree of sourness it is put into the refrigerator to maintain this level.

tomato

yogurt

vinegar

tamarind

fish tamarind

lime

cocum

mango

kaachri

pomegranate seeds

mango powder

sun-dried raw mango

Vinegar

Vinegar in cooking is found primarily in the regions of India influenced by the Portuguese—Goa, Mangalore, Kerala—as well as in Anglo-Indian and Parsee cooking. The Indians of the West coast use a vinegar made of coconut—the closest equivalent in the West would be cider vinegar. The Parsees use molasses vinegar made from sugar cane.

Tamarind

The most popular souring agent in Southern India is the tamarind fruit, which grows on a large graceful tree. The pods are collected, de-seeded, and dried. Before cooking the acid flesh is soaked in water, and the juice is squeezed out. It is this tamarind water that is used in the curry. In some Goan and Mangalorian recipes, the tamarind flesh is ground together with spices. Tamarind can be bought in any Indian grocer's and some supermarkets.

Lime

India is the original home of both the lime and the lemon, but nowadays it is the lime that is most commonly available and used, although limes are often called lemons. Thus, a so-called fresh lemon squash would actually be based on lime juice. In Hindi the lime is called the *nimbu* and is used in some curry dishes. The juice of the *nimbu* is added only at the end of the cooking process, as it would inhibit the meat from becoming tender while cooking.

Cocum

The cocum, which grows on trees along the Western coast of India, has a deep purple flesh surrounding a large seed. It imparts a pale-purplish color to food as well as a sour taste. It is used by Sindhis in their gram flour curry, and by the Hindu Goans in their fish curries. It is also made into sherbets on the West coast of India: these refreshing drinks are made from fruits, essences and herbs, for example, raw mango, fresh lime, lychees, almonds, and rose. Cocum has a remarkable anti-allergic action, and cocum-infused water drunk for three days first thing in the morning is said to cure urticaria or hives.

Raw mango

Mangoes (*kairi*) grow all over India in the summer. For two to three months before that, from about mid-March, the markets are full of bright green unripe mangoes of myriad varieties. These are used to make pickles and chutneys and finely chopped as a seasoning. During the spring "cheeks" of raw mango are put into curries and dals as souring agents. Raw mango cheeks are also sun-dried and powdered and in this state are called *amchoor* (*aamb* meaning mango and *choor* powder). *Amchoor* is only used as a garnish, for sprinkling on fried vegetable savories (*chaat*) or dal. It is not used during cooking.

the use of spices

Curry powder in the form that it is known now in the West, was invented in Madras, to be exported to England for use by the English who had become addicted, as we have already seen, to curries. In India, spices are used in a highly individual way, and daughters learn how to use them by observing their mothers or grandmothers. Each region of India and each sub-cuisine has its own traditional palette of spices. Professional cooks in India have a great understanding of the role, possible uses, and limitations of each spice. For example, pepper is used to much better effect in Kerala and the extreme south of India where it grows, while essence of the keora flower is a prized characteristic of Lucknowi cooking.

Incidentally, contrary to a widely held belief, various forms of curry powder do feature in the traditions of Indian cooking. Throughout the Western part of Maharashtra, masala powder (see pages 48–49) is ground and kept for later use, though the composition of the powder varies. The *kaala masala* or black masala powder used in many dishes consists of pepper, clove, cinnamon, and other black spices.

The East Indian Christian communities of Mumbai and Bassein make a curry powder comprising about thirty spices, some very little known. Unlike commercial curry powder, it resolves the problem of some spices getting cooked while others remain under-cooked, because each spice is roasted separately for different requisite lengths of time before grinding. They make it just before the hot season and store it, tightly packed into long green bottles, for a whole year. For this reason the mixture is called "bottled masala", although it is in fact a curry powder. Similarly, in March and April the Chettiars of Tamil Nadu sun-dry several spices, and onions as well, and make little marble-sized balls of curry powder rolled with oil which they also store for the entire year. These are called *kaarivadagam*: the addition of oil helps them to keep longer.

By and large, however, spices are used individually in Indian cooking. In previous centuries spices were prized for their preservative and medicinal qualities. But today dried spices are used principally for their taste and aroma in cooking and their digestive properties.

Grinding spices

This is a very important part of the curry-making process. If the spices are not ground properly the curry will have neither the correct texture nor taste. In the old days, every large household's cook had an assistant in the kitchen known as a *masaalchi*, who ground all the spice mixtures. In Indian restaurants and hotel kitchens, professional cooks guard their recipes for spice mixtures closely, putting their own proportions of the spices into grinders for apprentices to oversee.

Every home in India, however lowly, has a grinding stone. This is a piece of black granite and comes with a thick version of a rolling pin. In some parts of Southern India, the grinding stone is like a round basin with the centre scooped out and then the end of the rolling pin is used to crush the spices. A lot of pressure is required to grind the spices to a smooth, fine consistency. Most Indians will tell you there is a vast difference in the taste between spices ground on a stone and those made in an electric mixer. A small version of the stone grinder with an electric motor is available and is principally used in Southern India to grind rice and lentils for making *idlis* and *dosas* (items in a Southern Indian breakfast), and not so much to grind spices for curries.

In the last decade or so, a good range of electrical kitchen gadgets such as liquidizers especially suited to the preparation of Indian food has become available in India. The blades of these machines are close to the base, which enables the spices to be ground more finely than in Western grinders. Liquidizers come with two sizes of bowl, one with a very small capacity for spices and a larger one for coconut and large quantities of ingredients. The appliances do not heat up quickly as the motors are heavy-duty and therefore the spices can be ground for 10–15 minutes without a problem.

When selecting an appliance for grinding, a coffee grinder is useful for day-to-day grinding of spices and should be kept specifically for that purpose. For what Indians call "wet grinding", that is, items like coconut where a little liquid is added, you need to buy a medium-sized machine with blades close to the base of the machine. This also applies to red chiles or they will not be ground to a smooth paste. Soften the chile skins by soaking in water for 30 minutes and they will grind much better. Small herb mills are fine for grinding ginger, garlic, green chile, and cilantro leaves.

spices used mainly for taste

Coriander seeds and coriander powder (*dhania*)

The principal spice in this category is coriander powder. This is made by grinding coriander seeds. To enhance the flavor the seeds should be roasted on a hot *tawa* or griddle or skillet without oil for 3 minutes or so, and ground just before use. This can be done in a dry grinder or coffee grinder kept specially for this purpose. Housewives and professional cooks who are particular about the taste of their curries, roast and grind coriander powder every day. Frying the coriander powder in oil gives the characteristic "curry" flavor. It takes a minimum of 5 minutes cooking in hot oil over a low heat for the full flavor to be released from the spice into the mixture. Adding a tablespoon or two of water will not inhibit the release of flavor. Frying over a high heat means the powder will burn and become sticky more quickly. It tends to catch on the bottom of the pan unless there is a substantial amount of oil or fat, and therefore needs to be stirred continuously. If meat is being fried along with the powder, then one can stir-fry or bhuna the meat with powder for as long as 10 minutes without burning because there is moisture in the meat. This is the characteristic taste of a *bhuna* dish.

Coriander seeds have diuretic properties. Coriander is grown all over India but Rajasthan and Central India produce the most. The Rajasthan variety, which is lighter brown in color, is also the most flavorful with a good aroma. It is mostly this variety that is used in India to make commercial coriander powder. The coriander from around Indore in Central India has a greenish tinge and is mostly used in seed form. The coriander sold in the U.S. is also imported from North Africa and Eastern Europe.

Turmeric (*haldi*)

This is a root and is mostly used as a powder made from the dried root. Fresh turmeric root, available from December to March in India, gives an even better color and flavor than dried. Turmeric is difficult to powder at home, and there is always a danger of buying an adulterated form in markets, so shrewd housewives buy their annual requirements before the summer and get it pounded in their presence. Turmeric has antiseptic qualities and is therefore used to marinate fish before cooking, particularly by the Hindus. In the making of curries, turmeric is used more by the Hindus than the Muslims, who avoid using it in many recipes. It sticks very easily to the bottom of the pan during frying, but needs only a few seconds of frying to release its flavor, does not burn quickly and can therefore be added at any point in the frying sequence, even if only spices are being fried, without meat, fish, or vegetables. The largest turmeric production is around the town of Erode in Tamil Nadu, in Andhra and Maharashtra. That which gives the brightest hue is from the area around Allepey in Kerala. The biggest turmeric market in the world is in Sangli, where the turmeric is stored in large pits in the ground.

Dried red chile and chile powder

These are explained in detail in a separate section. When adding chile powder in a curry recipe, do so during the second half of the frying sequence if only spices are fried, as within a few seconds or so chile emits

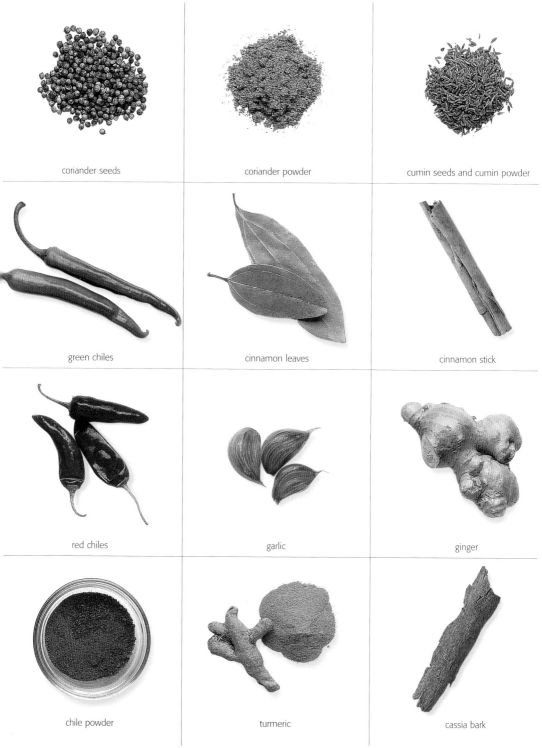

coriander seeds

coriander powder

cumin seeds and cumin powder

green chiles

cinnamon leaves

cinnamon stick

red chiles

garlic

ginger

chile powder

turmeric

cassia bark

pungent vapors which make you cough. Fried with meat or chicken it can comfortably be cooked along with other spices like coriander and turmeric for 10 minutes. If you are frying chile on its own and get a singeing aroma, add a little water.

Cumin seeds (*jeera*)
Cumin seeds are used whole or ground as powder. Again, they should be roasted very briefly for less than a minute on a hot *tawa* or griddle and then ground into a powder to release their flavor more fully. Whole or powdered *jeera* burns quicker than most spices, turns black quickly and becomes bitter, and should therefore be fried for less than half a minute or until you see it is turning a blackish color, at which point add the next ingredient, be it tomato, yogurt, or any other ingredient containing moisture. This will stop the burning process. Cumin seeds are used in the cooking of dry vegetable dishes like *jeera aloo* (with potatoes). Fried in a little oil and made into a *wagar* or seasoning, the seeds are sprinkled on top of boiled rice or dal.

Cumin is considered to be a digestive. The drink known as *jeera paani* or cumin water, is basically an infusion of cumin, lime juice, and fresh cilantro leaves. It also has "cooling" properties.

Cinnamon and cloves (*tuj/dalchini* and *lavang*)
These spices contribute to both taste and aroma but have a specially strong impact on taste. They are used whole in some meat recipes, and along with green cardamom when boiling rice to make a simple pulao, or ground together with black cardamom and made into a garam masala powder (see pages 48–49). Commercial garam masala powder exists but is by no means always ideal, because many manufacturers tend to skimp on using the expensive ingredients and add inessential cheaper ones to increase the volume. Many housewives prefer the flavor of home-made garam masala.

Cinnamon is a thinner, tan-colored bark, while cassia is a rougher, dark brown bark. Often what is sold in the name of cinnamon is actually cassia bark, so be sure to buy a good brand of cinnamon. Cassia has a sweeter taste than cinnamon.

The whole spices can be fried for a few minutes without burning. Cinnamon can be fried for 5 minutes, and cloves for under 2 minutes if there are no other ingredients with moisture. If roasting them dry in a powdered form with other spices, allow under 2 minutes over a low heat.

It is not essential that cinnamon and cloves be fried, though this releases the flavor better into the oil. They can, however, be successfully added directly to a curry or rice mixture. Clove is a strong spice, and just 2 or 3 in a dish give a perceptible flavor. Cloves burn faster than cinnamon, and should always be put in after cinnamon.

Pepper (*kali mirchi*)

Pepper grows mainly in Kerala. It was a highly prized item in world trade as far back as the second century AD, when pepper from Malabar was exported to Rome in exchange for gold. Christopher Colombus set off on his journey of discovery in search of the source of pepper and cloves. In those days pepper was especially prized for its preservative qualities.

Peppercorns boiled in water along with Indian basil leaves (*tulsi*) is drunk in India as an infusion to cure a cold in the chest or asthma. Pepper is used lavishly in Kerala cooking. When frying, the peppercorn is always used whole and should be fried for not more than 1 minute, if no other ingredient with moisture is present.

In India, spices cooked whole do not dissolve during the cooking of a curry, and Indians are quite used to them appearing on their plate or in their mouths and will discreetly put them aside. They can be tied in a muslin bag during cooking and removed from the pan after frying.

Mustard seeds (*rai* or *sarson*)

Mustard seeds are used whole in Southern Indian curries and vegetable dishes, almost always as the first ingredient to be fried for a few seconds in the cooking oil. Mustard seeds are the favorite spice of Bengal, where mustard grows in abundance; the seeds are ground into a paste and used to flavor Bengali fish dishes. Mustard oil is also widely used in Bengal and Kashmir. In the Punjab, the leaves of the mustard plant are a favorite winter vegetable.

If frying mustard seeds whole, do so for 10–15 seconds when they will begin to splutter and crackle. Then add the next spice or ingredient according to the recipe. In Indian cooking the use of mustard powder or prepared mustard is insignificant, though the latter, if added, to some curry preparations could enhance the taste. So feel free to innovate.

The most commonly used mustard seeds are black (*rai*), though in the north and east of the country, reddish-brown ones (*sarson*) are used.

Fenugreek seeds (*methi*)

These are usually used whole, and only in a few recipes. In Southern Indian cuisine, *methi* seeds are the second ingredient after mustard seeds to be put in hot oil and fried for a few seconds before the other ingredients are added. They are also used roasted and powdered along with red chile and other spices in a condiment mix known as *muligapuri*, to be eaten with *idli* and *dosas*.

Poppy seeds (*khus khus*)

These are almost always used in a curry ground to a paste with a little water. They do not grind easily and should be lightly toasted on a griddle for 3–4 minutes, then ground in a coffee grinder with a little water added if necessary. They have a very mild flavor. Used as a coating for potatoes and fried savoury items they impart a nutty taste, as they do to curry, in which they are used as a thickening agent.

Fennel (*saunf*)

This sometimes forms part of garam masala powder. Fennel powder features in Kashmiri cuisine, both Hindu and Muslim, and is also used by the Mapla Muslims of Kerala. It is not essential to fry fennel powder as it is very aromatic. In Kashmiri curries, fennel powder is always used without the frying process. In Chettinad cuisine whole fennel seeds are used as one of the main spices.

Many Indian cookery books mention aniseed as a spice, but actually it is fennel that is being referred to–aniseed is not used in Indian cuisine.

spices used mainly for aroma

It is very difficult to distinguish spices used principally for taste and those for aroma, as all spices will affect both. However, some have a marginally greater effect on taste and others on aroma, and for those who are not very familiar with spices, this distinction can help to make it easier to appreciate the role of each spice a little better. Some, like the garam masala spices, affect taste if fried in the initial mixture, but contribute to the aroma in a stronger way if sprinkled on in powder form towards the end of the cooking process. The spices which contribute more to aroma are detailed in this section.

Garam masala

As mentioned above, garam masala contributes to both flavor and aroma, but I feel the latter is predominant. *Garam* means "heating" in this context (though in Hindi the literal translation is "hot"). *Masala*, of course, refers to the spices. So garam masala is a mixture of those spices which create heat in the body—cinnamon, cloves, black pepper, and black cardamom. Interestingly, the first two were exported to India at the time of the spice trade! Nowadays housewives making garam masala mixture sometimes include the "cooling" green cardamom, the *tej patta* or Indian bay leaf, and fennel (*saunf*). Master chefs use a wide array of spices, including dried rose petals. Every recipe for garam masala powder is different. To get the best flavor, grind a small quantity in a coffee grinder just before use.

garam masala powder

commercial whole garam masala mix

cloves

cinnamon

large black cardamom

black peppercorns

Garam masala is used mostly with meat and to a lesser extent in poultry and rice dishes. It is rarely used in fish or vegetable dishes because its aroma is considered to be too strong for these.

Making your own garam masala
Indian housewives always buy whole garam masala spices (cinnamon sticks, cloves, peppercorns and black cardamom pods, sometimes cumin and coriander seeds), then toast them on a griddle and pound them into a powder in a mortar with a pestle. Nowadays, Indian food processors have a small attachment (like a coffee grinder) for dry-grinding small quantities of spices, so pounding is no longer necessary.

There are two ways to make your own. One is to buy everything whole and proceed as above. Or you can buy everything ready-powdered, and mix the spices thoroughly in a bowl with a spoon.

A classic garam masala would have approximately equal quantities in weight of cinnamon, cloves and black pepper, with a little black cardamom. The rest depends on individual preference. I like to add fennel seeds and a touch of cinnamon leaf.

So, if using whole spices, take 6 grams of cinnamon (this is a lot of cinnamon, which is very light), 6 grams each of cloves and pepper, and 1 black cardamom (2 grams). You can add 1 teaspoon of fennel seeds and 1 cinnamon or bay leaf.

Alternatively, take $2^1/_2$ teaspoons of cinnamon powder, 1 teaspoon each of clove powder and black pepper, and $^3/_4$ teaspoon of fennel powder. Then grind one black cardamom and a cinnamon or bay leaf together and add this powder to the mixture.

Store garam masala in a tightly sealed bottle in the refrigerator, where it will keep for 6 months if you have used fresh spices to start with, though in terms of flavor, it is better to use it within 3 months.

Cinnamon leaf (*tej* or *tuj patta*)
Tej in Hindi means sharp and *patta* means leaf. So it is presumed in India that *tej patta* refers to the leaf with a sharp and strong flavor. But *tej* is actually a corruption of the word *tuj* in Gujarati (the language used in Mumbai, India's largest spice city) which means cinnamon, so *tej patta* is the cinnamon-flavored leaf from a tree which is similar to the cinnamon tree.

Cinnamon is part of the same botanical family *Lauraceae* as the Mediterranean bay tree (the *Laurus nobilis*) but true cinnamon is *Cinnamomum zeylenicum*; cassia, which is similar in flavor to cinnamon, is *Cinnamomum aromaticum*; and the *tej patta* leaf is *Cinnamomum tamala*. It grows in north-east India, and in Kerala.

The *tej patta* leaf is usually fried in the initial stages of making a curry and does not burn even if fried over a low to medium heat for 10 minutes, as it browns and releases its flavor gradually. It can also be put in a boiling gravy or rice. Before serving remove it from the cooking pot.

The Indian cinnamon leaf is not presently available in the West, but the Mediterranean bay leaf can be used in its place.

Large black cardamom (*barra elaichi*)
Barra means large and this cardamom is about 6–8 times the size of the small green cardamom. Black cardamom is used only in Indian curries, and is grown in north-east India and Sikkim. It has a strong aroma, the flavor being in its seeds. It is used in small quantities and should form a part of any recipe for garam masala powder.

If black cardamom is used whole it should be removed from the pot before serving. If only the seeds are used, pound before using and they will dissolve into the food during cooking. Black cardamom, featured in several recipes in this book, is available from Indian grocery shops.

Green cardamom (*elaichi* powder)
Green cardamom, apart from having a unique aroma, also contributes to flavor. Avoid using white cardamom which is a bleached version of the green variety and has less flavor. Powder made from the whole green cardamom, sprinkled at the end of the cooking process on a delicate lamb or mutton dish just a few minutes before serving, gives a wonderful aroma (the dish should be kept covered). This can be done even if whole or crushed cardamoms have already been used in the cooking, because by the end, when a number of spices have been used, no single aroma will predominate.

Cardamom in crushed form is also used in sweet dishes like *shrikand* (flavoured hung yogurt), and in cooling drinks like the almond-flavored *thandai*. Cardamom has cooling properties even though some housewives put it in their garam masala.

asafoetida

caraway seeds

fenugreek seeds

white poppy seeds

cumin seeds

green cardamom

wild onion seeds

fennel seeds

mace

triphala

nutmeg

star anise

dried rose petals

black mustard seeds

yellow mustard seeds

Nutmeg (*jaiphal*)

Nutmeg originates from the Moluccas in Indonesia and in earlier times was exported to India. Today it is grown in Kerala.

Nutmeg is used sparingly in Indian cooking, in both curries and sweet dishes. Always used in its powdered form, it is normally added during the cooking process, and is not fried along with the main spices. Try putting *jaiphal* powder on puréed spinach—it transforms the dish.

Mace Powder (*javitri*)

Mace is the net-like covering of nutmeg. Like cardamom, powdered mace gives a wonderful aroma when sprinkled on meat dishes towards the end of cooking, and on pulao dishes in which rice is cooked along with the other main ingredient, for example lamb or mixed vegetables. It is a favorite condiment among the Muslim court cooks of Lucknow, who use it during the cooking of hot kormas as well as sprinkling it on the top when the dish is almost ready. It is important to keep the lid on, so that the aroma is incorporated in the dish, aided by the heat within.

Asafoetida (*hing*)

This is a seasoning used primarily as an anti-flatulent, and has a strong aroma. It is a resin from the plant *Ferula asafoetadia*, imported mainly from Iran. Minute quantities are used in cooking.

Star aniseed (*chakraphool* or *badian*)

This is native to China and is not commonly used in Indian cooking. Its widest use is in Kashmir and Chettinad cooking—the Chettiar community of the south-east coast of India traded with China and South West Asia for many hundreds of years. It is also incorporated in the east Indian bottled masala, and in a few Goan dishes.

Saffron (*kesar*)

Saffron has a delicate fragrance, and is the most expensive spice in the world. It is the stigma of a flower of the crocus family which originated in west Asia and grows in Kashmir and Turkey, and in Mediterranean countries—the largest quantity now comes from Spain. The use of saffron is very much part of Indian cooking, especially in Moghlai dishes since it was a favorite ingredient in the Moghul courts. It is now popular in India for biryanis, pulaos, *kesari* chicken (a creamy saffron curry dish), and desserts such as *kesari kulfi*. Saffron comes in strands which need to be soaked in a little warm water or milk to infuse. It also gives off a golden-yellow dye which imparts a pale yellow hue to white rice or a milk-based dessert. It loses its flavor after a month, and is best stored tightly sealed in a refrigerator.

Powdered rose petals (*gulab*)

Powdered rose petals are used for their aroma and marinade qualities when cooking meat dishes. This tradition can be seen today in the Lucknowi court dishes, particularly in light-colored delicate kormas such as the white korma (see page 104). The Indian rose is small with a double row of petals, and has a much more intense fragrance than Western roses. The best-quality Indian roses for culinary purposes are the small ones (*gulabs*) from the Udaipur region (where they were specially cultivated to make a rose liqueur called *Gulab*), from Mysore and near Kanauj in North India.

The rose petals are sun-dried and then powdered for use in cooking. *Gulab* has cooling properties, and is also astringent and anti-inflammatory. Rose essence is used in making sherbets. Rose water is used for sprinkling, after cooking, on biryanis and pulaos, and also for soaking saffron.

Screwpine flower essence (*Keora* essence)

Pandanus odoratissimus is a yellow flower from the screwpine family, with a very strong, sweet aroma. The male flowers are valued for their fragrance. It grows in Orissa and to a lesser degree in Kerala. *Keora* (sometimes spelt as *Kewda*) *attar* and *Keora* water are made using an extraction of this flower. *Keora* oil is believed to be a stimulant.

Keora attar is made for culinary purposes in Lucknow, and just a drop diluted in a little water before using is enough to flavor 2¼lb of meat. A more diluted version of this is *Keora* water. Lucknow cooks use it in biryanis, kebabs, and kormas, and are now being imitated by Muslim cooks all over India.

Screwpine flower

herbs and fresh spices

The term *hara masala*, meaning literally "green spices", refers to fresh ginger, garlic, green chiles, fresh cilantro leaves, curry leaves, fenugreek leaves, mint, lime, scallions, and any other herbs, such as fresh dill. Most curries will contain *hara masala* in one form or another. In the vegetable markets there are vendors who specialize only in the sale of these herbs.

Almost all curry recipes include ginger and garlic. The traditional method is to chop them finely and fry them along with the onions. They are usually used together, often in almost equal quantities. Someone once explained to me that this is because, while ginger tends to raise blood pressure, garlic is good for keeping it low, and so both are used to maintain an even keel. I do not know how much credence can be given to this theory, but there it is.

Professional restaurant cooks now make a purée of equal quantities of ginger and garlic either together or separately, and this can be stored in a refrigerator (covered, please remember) for several days. Housewives are increasingly beginning to do the same for the sake of convenience.

There are two varieties of garlic in India which I have not seen anywhere else. One is called *taaza lasan* (fresh garlic) and is a plant about 7-in high with a single garlic clove at the tip of its root. Very popular in Mumbai in the winter, it is used by the Sindhis to flavor fish dishes, by the Parsees in scrambled egg, and in mincemeat by the Boris. It is the young shoots of the normal garlic plant grown in sandy soil. Another form of garlic is a tiny bead-like pod which the vegetable sellers say is good for the heart!

Ginger is almost always used fresh—it keeps well for a couple of months, particularly in a cold place. Powdered ginger is used mostly in Kashmir and in *chaat* preparations in North India.

fenugreek

dill

red chiles

cilantro

garlic

whole pod garlic

fresh garlic

kashmiri shallots

green chiles

african chiles

curry leaves

ginger

fresh mint

Fresh cilantro leaves are used both as an ingredient at the beginning of cooking and at the end as a decorative and aromatic garnish. They are also one of the main ingredients in a green curry. Cilantro leaves, mint, ginger, lime juice, and sugar blended together in a mixer makes a delicious fresh green chutney.

Mint is used in cooking, particularly in making *dhansak* and biryani, but is added towards the end in order to retain the flavor. Mint should not be fried with the masala as it turns black quite quickly and will give a blackish color to the curry.

Curry leaf is a herb used only in Southern and Western coast cooking of India from Mumbai down to Kerala, though it is absent in Goan cooking. It is very fragrant and can be fried in the initial stages or put in at the simmering stage. Added at the final stage of a curry, it will retain maximum flavor, but it needs to cook for at least 5 minutes. It is used in dry dishes, dals, *khadis*, in yogurt and vegetable dishes, in meat curries, and in some fish curries of Kerala and Madras. When dried, the curry leaves have very little flavor.

Curry leaf is from the same botanical family as the *neem* tree, the leaves of which have anti-bacterial properties, and is used as a natural pesticide.

Fenugreek (*methi*) leaves are used only in Indian cooking. There are two varieties of *methi*—the small one, about 3-in high with tiny bud-like leaves, has a more delicate flavor but has a very short season in the summer. The larger *methi* leaf is about 10-in high and is available throughout the year. It is very easy to grow from seed. The small *methi* is actually the young shoots of the larger *methi*, but grown in sandy soil. It has a far more intense and fragrant flavor and is available only in Mumbai and Western India.

Methi leaves have a unique flavor with a slightly bitter tinge and are an acquired taste. A favorite Indian dish is *methi aloo*, or potatoes made in quite dry *karai* flavored with *methi*. A recipe is given in this book (see page 185). *Methi* leaves are used throughout India. The Punjabis put it in many dishes, including Chicken Makhani, the Parsees use it in *dhansak*, and the favorite Sindhi style of preparing fish is with fresh single-cloved garlic (they call it *thoom*) and *methi* leaves.

Methi is also sold dried, in packets known as *kasuri methi*, in most Indian grocery shops. It is quite strong in flavor, and only a pinch of it should be used in a dish. The dry *methi* is not the same botanical species as the fresh one.

Dill (*sooaa*) is used to flavor spinach and other leafy green vegetables, and *dhansak*. The Sindhis have a green spinach dish known as *sai bhaji* and also make a dill-flavored rice, for which the recipe is also given in this book (see page 173).

chiles

It is important to understand the use of chiles in the making of curries, since they are an important ingredient and their use is limited in the West. Chiles are becoming increasingly popular in some parts of America however, largely because of the influence of Mexican cuisine, in which a variety of chiles are used.

In Indian cooking two kinds of chile are used—the green variety which is used fresh and the red, used in dried form. The varieties of green chile differ in their size (length) and pungency. Therefore, quantities of green chiles in a recipe are only indicative. If a curry is meant to be pungent the recipe will say so, and if the particular chiles you are using are not very hot, you should increase the number, and vice versa.

Chiles are always most pungent when raw, and mellow when fried or braised. Therefore, though the recipes may appear to contain many chiles, the finished dishes will not be as hot as they first appeared. Chiles are a valuable source of vitamin C and are good for digestion. In India they are eaten raw, as in a cachumber salad or a fresh green chutney, as well as cooked, and are included in almost all savory preparations. The closest American chile to the Indian green one is the Sertano.

Red chiles are sometimes used in addition to green chiles in curries, for their hot taste and to give a reddish color. On the western and southern coasts of India the skin of the red chile is ground together with coconut to give the curry texture.

The correct use of red chiles is vital if one wants to make gourmet-style curries. The Indian housewife cooks in the culinary style of her own region and when shopping buys the locally available chile, without perhaps being aware of its origin. It was only when I began to cook the recipes that I had gathered from different parts of India in my kitchen in Mumbai that I realised that the original taste was missing and that this difference was due to the variation in chiles used elsewhere in the country. But cookery books, restaurants, and home cooks in India rarely specify the use of different chiles in the different regional recipes. The only exception is the so-called **Kashmiri chile** which is often mentioned because in recent years it has become popular as the variety

chile powders

| hot chile powder | paprika (mild) | red chile powder | cayenne | paprika (hot) | kashmiri chile powder |

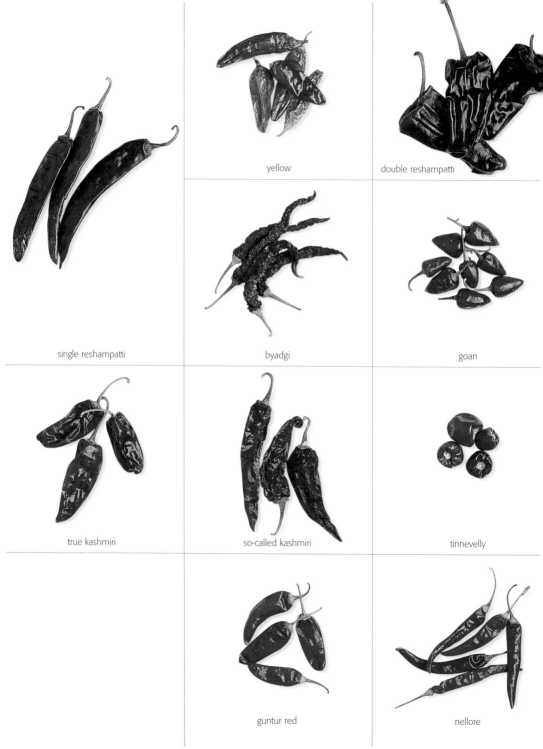

yellow

double reshampatti

single reshampatti

byadgi

goan

true kashmiri

so-called kashmiri

tinnevelly

guntur red

nellore

that gives bright red color and at the same time is mildly hot in taste. I say "so-called" because when I tried to trace the origin of the Kashmiri chile in the wholesale chile markets in India, I found that Kashmir itself did not export the quantities of Kashmiri chiles being sold everywhere, and a similar variety was being cultivated in northern Karnataka, the region east of Goa, and in Andhra, and was widely sold all over India as Kashmiri chile! So, if substituting the Kashmiri chile, look for the type that is the length of a finger and gives more bright red color than "bite". The New Mexico chile is a good substitute, though its powder or purée does not have the bright color of the Indian Kashmiri type.

India is the largest world producer of chiles, with annual production in the order of 80,000 tonnes: only about 25,000 tonnes are exported. There is a growing export trade of spice oils and oleoresins (essential extracts) of chiles for the bulk food business, for which chiles with the best color are used. Chiles are grown throughout the country for local use, but for cash crops the largest producers are Maharashtra, Tamil Nadu (the Madras variety), Andhra (the Guntur variety being the most pungent and therefore largely used for commercially sold red chile powder), Karnataka (the Bedgi and Kashmiri variety), and Rajasthan. Kashmir grows its bright red and fragrant chiles largely for home consumption, as the hilly terrain makes it commercially unviable to transport it. Goa also grows its own large-size chile, which is ideal for the Goa curry, but even the Goans have developed a fascination for using the Kashmiri variety. The gourmets of Northern India use a bright yellow dried chile grown around the Sonepat area in Punjab for their white or yellow curry dishes.

Recipes indicate whether green chiles are to be used whole, slit or chopped, as the manner of cutting the chile affects the pungency of the curry. A slit chile imparts some pungency to the curry, the whole chile much less. Some dishes call for broken-up red chile, others for it to be ground into a paste with a little water or vinegar, while in other recipes only red chile powder is used. The stalks of chiles are always removed before use.

To achieve the bright color effect of red chile powder with a less hot taste, it can be mixed with paprika. Similarly, to reduce the pungency of red or green chiles, de-seed them before using. Remember to do this under running water, using gloves if your hands are sensitive, and to wash your hands thoroughly with soap immediately afterwards.

The recipes in this book mention the use of a particular chile if it is vital to the taste. I hope that before long grocery shops and supermarkets outside India will become increasingly particular about the chiles they sell, and manufacturers will respond to the market and supply the chile variety specified, both whole and in powdered form.

the curry picture

Starting Point	Name of Curry	Color	Thickening Agent	Dominant Spice
Want to have a mild fish curry.	Fish curry in coconut milk – fish molee	Pale yellow	Coconut milk	Ginger
Want to have lamb to eat with sliced bread.	Seyal Gosht	Light brown	Onions and yogurt	Cilantro
Want to have a mild chicken curry without coconut to have with rice and/or roti.	Kashmiri Chicken Korma	Ochre	Onion	Cardamom Cinnamon
Want to combine meat or chicken with lentils and vegetables, eat it with rice and not have to make a side dish. Also should be able to keep it in a fridge for the next day.	Dhansak	Deep greenish brown	Lentils	Cilantro Cumin powder
Want to make a simple curry to cater for both vegetarians and non-vegetarians without having to make two recipes.	Goa curry – seafood or chicken and mixed veg.	Orangey red	Ground coconut	Coriander seeds Chile

Supporting Spice	Souring Agent	Chile to be used	To be eaten with
Cloves Cinnamon Cardamom	–	Slit green chiles	White rice Tomato rice Green rice
Whole cloves Cinnamon Cardamom	Yogurt and tomatoes	Fresh green and red chile powder	Pulao rice or sliced bread or paratha
Ginger powder Cloves	Yogurt	Green chiles	Any rice or roti
Fenugreek leaves Cloves Cinnamon	Lime juice Tamarind	Fresh green and red chile powder	Brown pulao rice Green coconut chutney Onion and tomato cachumber Fried papadums
Cilantro Turmeric	Tamarind (can also use vinegar)	Bright red Kashmiri type, dried red chile or red chile powder and paprika powder	White rice

hints and short cuts

Cut and prepare all the ingredients before you begin to cook. In Indian food particularly, there are so many ingredients that it is useful if they can be kept ready to use. If you have a large herb and spice collection, take out the ones needed for the dish in question and keep them handy.

If you are cooking for a party you can cook the curry and the dal a day ahead, though the dal should not be seasoned until shortly before serving. The vegetables can be cut and kept aside, a day in advance, but ideally should be cooked not more than a few hours beforehand. The same applies to the raita, for which the yogurt should be fresh. The bread dough for the rotis can be made a day ahead. The rotis themselves can be made a couple of hours ahead, spread with a little butter and wrapped in kitchen foil, then reheated in an oven just before serving. The chutney can be made a day ahead and stored in the refrigerator, though tomato chutney can be kept for a week. The cachumber should be made just about an hour before the party, and the papadams cooked.

Curries of meat and chicken can be successfully frozen, but the texture of cooked fish suffers a little. Cooked lentils, chickpeas, and vegetables freeze well.

If you are short of time and want to cook very quickly without having to peel and cut, use bottled ginger and garlic purée (the latter comes in tubes too), canned tomato purée, and canned cream of coconut where the recipe demands it. However, there is no short-cut for browned onions except to fry them in batches and freeze them.

Many housewives in India and outside peel and purée ginger and garlic, sometimes green chile too, and store it in jars in the refrigerator, which enables them to cook in a hurry.

Avoid using a sweet variety of onions. It is important that the moisture content is not too high—the ones in India are ripened fast and do not have a sweet taste. The recipes in this book have been adapted for onions grown in the West; those to avoid particularly are the sweet Spanish varieties.

Most of the recipes mention fresh tomatoes. If using canned tomatoes, they will give a better color to the curry, but you may have to increase the quantity of the souring ingredient if there is one in the curry and also the salt and chile, if necessary.

mishaps

1 If the onions burn while browning, remove all the burnt bits, change the pot and add a little fresh oil, otherwise the burnt taste will pervade the curry. You may have to start again.

2 If the curry has become too hot, and contains tomatoes and/or whipped yogurt, or coconut milk, add an extra tomato or two. Also add $1/2$–1 teaspoon of sugar. If the curry is a sour one, increase the souring agent.

3 If the curry has become too salty, add pieces of potato, or a piece of dough which you must remove before serving. The potatoes and dough will absorb the liquid and then you can top up with a cup of plain water which will dilute the saltiness.

4 If the curry is too liquid, boil uncovered (keep your extractor hood on!) for a few minutes.

5 If the curry is not spicy enough, fry whatever spices you like with some chopped green chile in hot oil in a little saucepan or ladle (be careful as the chile can splutter) and add to the curry.

Below: using a ladle to fry spices

making a simple homestyle curry

or the first lesson in making a curry

Before attempting the curry recipes in this book you may like to start with the simplest way of making a homestyle curry, as follows. You can substitute fresh ginger and garlic, with one teaspoon of bottled ginger/garlic purée. (If cooking for 1, put the remaining half in the fridge or freezer.)

Curry for 2

Chicken curry

1lb Cornish hen or
2 breast fillets or
4 thighs or
6 drumsticks

Lamb curry

10oz stewing lamb

Fish curry

2 fillets of cod, about 8oz, or
2 salmon steaks

Vegetable curry

8oz mixed diced vegetables

Curry sauce

4 tablespoons oil
1 large onion, very finely chopped
2 cloves garlic, chopped
$1/4$-in square piece of fresh ginger, chopped
$3/4$ teaspoon coriander powder
a pinch of turmeric powder
$1/4$ teaspoon cumin powder
$1/4$ teaspoon garam masala powder
1 teaspoon paprika powder
2 tomatoes, chopped
salt
chopped cilantro leaves to garnish

1 Heat the oil in a heavy pan. Add the onion and sauté over a medium heat for about 20–25 minutes or until deep brown. Add the garlic and ginger and fry for 1 minute. Add the coriander powder and stir for a further full minute. Then add the turmeric, cumin, garam masala, and paprika and sauté for 30 seconds. Add 1 cup of water and cook for 10 minutes. Put in the tomatoes, stir well, and cook for a further 5 minutes.

2 Now the curry sauce is ready. Add salt to taste. Put in the chicken, lamb, fish, or vegetables. Add 1$1/2$ cups of water for the chicken, 2$1/2$ cups for the lamb, 1 cup for the fish, 2 cups for the vegetables. Cook until done. Sprinkle with chopped cilantro leaves just before serving.

Eat with rice, pitta bread or on sliced bread.

Opposite: frying onions properly is one very important factor in curry-making

rogan josh *kashmir*

Rogan means meat fat and *josh* literally means heat, though figuratively it means intensity. Traditionally fatty meat on the bone was used for making *Rogan Josh* and slow-cooked in its own fat, with extra added for an intense flavor. These days, however, we avoid animal fat and use a minimum amount of oil. The dish gets its heat and intensity from the lavish use of body heat-inducing spices such as large black cardamoms and cloves.

The hallmark of the dish as cooked in Kashmir is the liberal use of the true Kashmiri red chile, which has a mild flavor but gives a bright red color. The Muslims there use *praan*, a Kashmiri shallot, that has a garlicky flavor, and *maval*, the petals of the cockscomb flower. The latter gives the curry an even brighter red color and is supposed to have cooling properties. The Hindus of Kashmir do not use *praan* or any onion or garlic, but give body or flavor to the curry by adding yogurt. The spice distinguishing Kashmiri *Rogan Josh* from those made in other parts of India is fennel powder. I have combined the recipes of both the Hindu and Muslim communities to create a curry that is mildly spicy with a ravishing flavor.

Serves 4

1 1/2 lb stewing lamb
  or chops
9oz lamb bones for
  adding flavor
4 cloves garlic, chopped
salt to taste–about 1 1/4
  teaspoons
2 1/2 teaspoons chile powder
  (preferably Kashmiri)
  or 2 teaspoons chile
  powder and 1 teaspoon
  paprika
1/2 cup plain yogurt
9oz shallots, chopped
1/4 cup ghee or oil
4 cloves
2 large black cardamoms
4 green cardamoms
2 cinnamon or bay leaves
1 blade of mace
1 teaspoon coriander powder
1 teaspoon fennel powder
1 teaspoon ginger powder
1/4 teaspoon turmeric powder

1 Boil the lamb and bones with the garlic and 1/2 teaspoon of salt in 6 cups of water in a cooking pot for 20 minutes. Remove from the heat. Remove the meat and set aside. Skim off the scum, strain, and reserve the cooking liquor.

2 Make a paste of chile powder and/or paprika by mixing with a little water. Whisk the yogurt and set aside.

3 Fry the shallots in the ghee or oil in a pot until lightly browned (this will take about 12 minutes). Add the cloves, cardamoms, cinnamon or bay leaves, and the mace, and fry for 1 minute. Then add the coriander, fennel, ginger and turmeric powders, chile paste, and 2 tablespoons of water and stir continuously. After 2 minutes add the meat. Sauté for about 5 minutes. Lower the heat and add the yogurt, stir well, and sauté for a few minutes.

4 Add salt to taste, together with 4 cups of water. Cook until the meat is tender. Before serving, remove the cinnamon or bay leaves, the large cardamoms and mace if intact.

This curry is traditionally eaten with boiled rice, but can also be eaten with rotis or a saffron pulao.

lamb with turnips (shalgam gosht) *kashmir*

In the winter in Kashmir, turnips *(shalgam)* with a lovely mauvish tinge are one of the few vegetables available. They are stored in pits dug in the snow. This variety of turnip is the size of a medium onion, and grows throughout north India. *Shalgam Gosht* is popular in Lucknow too.

The Kashmiri red chile gives the dish a wonderful red color, which can also be achieved by using a blend of red chile powder and good paprika, as a substitute. The large black cardamom, which is considered to be heat-producing in the body—good in the winter!—gives it a nice aroma, as does the powdered fennel. The salt rubbed on the turnips before frying removes their bitterish taste.

Serves 4

11oz small turnips
salt
14oz small onions
2 cloves garlic
1 x ¹/₂-in piece of fresh
ginger
1¹/₂ medium tomatoes
about 9oz lamb bones
  for stock
1 bay leaf
5 tablespoons oil
1 teaspoon red chile powder
1¹/₂ teaspoons paprika
  powder
1 teaspoon turmeric powder
³/₄ teaspoon fennel powder
1¹/₂ teaspoons coriander
  powder
2 black cardamoms
4 green cardamoms
1¹/₂-in cinnamon stick
1¹/₂lb stewing lamb,
  cut into pieces

1 Peel the turnips and cut into quarters. Prick each piece several times with a toothpick. Sprinkle with a little salt and rub in well. Leave at room temperature to degorge for at least 1 hour, then rinse off the salt and set the turnips aside.

2 Chop the onions, 1 clove of garlic, and the ginger. Cut the tomatoes in half and grate, discarding the skin. Alternatively purée the peeled tomatoes in a blender.

3 Make a stock by boiling the lamb bones for 45 minutes in 2 cups of water along with the remaining clove of garlic and the bay leaf, and strain.

4 In a skillet, heat 3 tablespoons of the oil and fry the turnips for about 20 minutes until they are pale gold in color and beginning to get a crispy skin. Keep turning them around so they become evenly pale gold in color. Remove the turnips and drain on kitchen paper.

5 Put the oil from the pan into a cooking pot. Add 1 tablespoon of the remaining oil. Add the chopped onions and sauté for about 20–25 minutes over a low to moderate heat until golden-brown. Make sure the heat is not too high or they will fry unevenly. Add the chopped ginger and garlic, and continue to sauté for a further 5 minutes.

6 Add the chile, paprika, turmeric, fennel and coriander powders, the cardamoms, cinnamon, 2 tablespoons of water, the remaining tablespoon of oil, and the lamb, and mix well. Stir-fry the meat for 2 minutes so that it is evenly coated with spices. Cover the pot and simmer for about 10 minutes until the meat releases moisture which mingles with the spices and is re-absorbed.

7 Remove lid when the meat is almost dry. Then, with a cooking spoon, stir and turn the meat over several times for 5 minutes. This continuous stirring enables the spice mixture around the meat to come into contact with the heat at the bottom of the pot, and gives the dish its special flavor. It is known as the *bhuna* process.

8 Season with 1 1/4 teaspoons of salt, add the puréed tomato, and again stir and turn the meat. Pour in the stock, cover the pan, and simmer for about 30 minutes. About 5 minutes before the meat is tender, add the turnips. Turn off the heat when the meat and turnips are tender. If the dish is not to be eaten for some time the turnips will continue to absorb some of the curry. So, when reheating, if more curry is desired just add extra water as required. Taste for seasoning, add more salt if necessary, and cook for a couple of minutes. Remove the bones before serving.

This curry is deep red in color but not as hot as it looks. If you want it hotter then increase the quantity of chile powder.

Duck and turnips are also cooked together in the same way in Kashmir. Instead of turnips you could use potatoes and the dish would be just as nice: you do not need to salt the potatoes.

lamb cooked in milk (aab gosht) *kashmir*

This is a Kashmiri Muslim recipe. *Aab* means water in Persian, and this curry has a watery consistency. A dish with the same name, but actually a different recipe, is made by the Muslims of Mumbai using coconut milk; as in kosher cooking, the Hindus do not cook meat and milk together.

This is one of the few curry recipes in which no chiles, ginger or garlic are used. It is fragrant and delicate in flavor, with a hint of sweetness. It can be fed even to a little child (in which case omit the white pepper). Eat with boiled rice, fragrant rice or rotis.

Serves 4

8 saffron strands
1 1/2lb stewing lamb
  or lamb chops, cubed
4oz shallots
4 tablespoons oil
9oz lamb bones for stock
salt
1 cinnamon leaf or bay leaf
2 cloves
6 green cardamoms
2 x 1 1/2-in cinnamon sticks
4 1/2 cups milk
2 tablespoons light cream
1 1/4 teaspoons fennel powder
1/2 teaspoon cumin powder
1/4 teaspoon ground white
  pepper
1/2 teaspoon sugar

1 Soak the saffron strands in 1/4 cup of water. Soak the lamb in lukewarm water for 30 minutes, until lightened in color.

2 Peel the shallots and purée in a food-processor, or grate them, and fry in 2 tablespoons of the oil in a skillet until golden.

3 Boil the meat and bones in a cooking pot in 6 cups of water, along with 3/4 teaspoon of salt, the cinnamon or bay leaf, 1 clove, 3 cardamoms, 1 cinnamon stick, and the fried shallots until tender. Lift out the meat and set aside. Strain the stock and discard the bones.

4 While the meat is cooking, bring the milk to boil in another pot, with the remaining clove, cardamoms, and cinnamon stick. Put a wooden spoon into the pot to prevent the milk boiling over. Stir from time to time and keep cooking until the milk reduces and thickens. When it is reduced by a third, remove from the heat and leave to cool. Strain. Add the cream and stir well. Now add the meat and 3 cups of the stock to the milk.

5 Heat the remaining oil in a ladle held over a moderate heat. Add the fennel powder to the oil, then after 20 seconds add the cumin and pepper. Fry for just 10 seconds, then pour the oil mixture into the meat. Add the sugar and milk, then season with salt to taste. Cook for a few minutes, with the lid on to prevent the meat from darkening.

6 To serve, reheat uncovered and simmer for about 2 minutes. Add the saffron just before removing from the heat.

If you require a little "pep" in the curry you can add a couple of slit green chiles during the last 10 minutes of the cooking time. Remove the chiles from the stock and add to the milk mixture.

lamb korma pilaf (korma pulao) *lucknow*

Lucknowi cuisine is a refined version of Moghul cuisine, with an accent on aromas, hence the mace, nutmeg, saffron and rosewater. Contrary to common belief, Lucknow is famous for its wide range of pulaos, rather than biryani. This pulao recipe is from the home of Bulu Hamied, who was born and raised in Lucknow.

Serves 6–8

14oz basmati rice

1¹/₃ cups oil

4 large onions, finely
  chopped

1 x ¹/₂-in piece of fresh
  ginger, peeled and chopped

6 cloves garlic, chopped

2 green chiles, chopped

5 cloves

5 cardamoms

2-in cinnamon stick,
  broken into pieces

2¹/₄lb boneless lamb

1 tablespoon coriander
  powder

¹/₂ teaspoon turmeric powder

1 level teaspoon cumin powder

1¹/₂ teaspoons red chile
  powder

3 pieces of mace

¹/₄ teaspoon nutmeg powder

3¹/₂oz plain yogurt
  (Greek yogurt)

2 tomatoes, chopped

1 teaspoon salt

For the rice

2 cassia leaves or bay leaves

1 teaspoon oil or butter

1 level teaspoon salt

a few strands of saffron

a few drops of rosewater
  (optional) or use milk

1 Wash the rice a couple of times, using fresh water each time. Leave the rice to soak in a bowl of water for 30 minutes.

2 Heat the oil in a shallow pot or large pan. Fry the onions until they are medium to darkish brown. Add the ginger, garlic, chiles, cloves, cardamoms, and cinnamon and fry for 2–3 minutes. Add the lamb and stir-fry over a low to medium heat, stirring continuously for at least 10–15 minutes. The longer you do so, the better the taste.

3 Add the coriander powder. Stir for 2 minutes, then add the other spice powders and mix well. Add ¹/₃ cup of water and stir. Let it simmer for 2 minutes.

4 Whisk or whip the yogurt with a fork and add to the pot. Add the tomatoes and salt. Stir, cover with a lid and leave to cook until the lamb is 90 per cent done, but checking every 15 minutes or so to see if the pot has dried up completely. If it does, add ¹/₂ cup of water or more. When the lamb is done, it should have a thick spice coating, but not a runny gravy.

5 Drain the rice and wash it well. Put into a separate pot with an equal quantity of water (measure using a cup or bowl). Put the same volume of water to boil with the bay leaves. When boiling, add the oil, salt, and turmeric. Then add the rice. Leave the pot uncovered. When the water is absorbed, the rice will be three-quarters cooked.

6 Soak the saffron in 2 tablespoons of rosewater and set aside.

7 Take a large ovenproof serving dish. Brush the bottom with a little oil. Put half the rice in and spread it evenly. Then put the cooked lamb on top and smooth over. Put the rest of the rice on top. Cover with a lid and cook in a preheated oven at 325°F for 20 minutes. The rice will have cooked and absorbed some of the moisture from the korma. You will also get a curried rice at the bottom and the fragrant rice at the top, making a delectable korma and rice combination. Sprinkle the saffron and rosewater or milk on top.

You can cook the rice and korma ahead of time, assemble in a serving dish and put in a preheated oven for 20 minutes. Serve immediately.

lamb with herbs and black pepper
(kaalee mirch cha mutton) *konkan coast*

This recipe is from the home of a chef from the Konkan coast. This region celebrates fresh cilantro leaves and, of course, pepper comes from from Calicut, just south of Goa. Don't be put off by the number of ingredients.

Serves 6

2 cups cilantro leaves

1/2 cup mint leaves

1/2 cup fresh grated coconut

about 20 skinned almonds or
   unroasted cashew nuts

6 green chiles

a pinch of mustard seeds or
   mustard powder or
   1/2 teaspoon mustard

4 tablespoons oil

3/4-in cinnamon stick, broken
   into pieces

4 green cardamom pods

3 cloves

7oz onions, finely chopped

4 cloves garlic, chopped

1 x 3/4-in piece of fresh ginger,
   peeled and chopped

2 1/4lb boneless stewing
   lamb, cut into 1-in cubes

1/2 teaspoon turmeric powder

1 1/2 teaspoons coriander powder

3/4 teaspoon cumin powder

3 1/2oz plain yogurt, whipped

salt

1 tablespoon lemon or lime
   juice

1 teaspoon freshly ground
   black pepper

1/2 teaspoon garam masala

1 tablespoon chopped
   cilantro leaves

1 Put the cilantro leaves, mint leaves, coconut, nuts, green chiles, and mustard into a food-processor and blend to a fine purée, adding 1/3 cup of water.

2 In a shallow pot, heat the oil, then add the cinnamon, cardamoms, and cloves. After 1 minute, add the onions and sauté for 15 minutes until the onions are just turning brown, then add the garlic, ginger, and the lamb. Turn the heat to medium-high and sauté the lamb for 5 minutes. Add the turmeric, coriander, and cumin powders, and stir the lamb continuously for a few minutes so that it is thoroughly coated with the spices.

3 Turn the heat down very low, then slowly add the yogurt and once again stir-fry for a couple of minutes. Add the green purée, 2 cups of water and 1 teaspoon of salt, bring to a boil, cover and leave to simmer for about 45 minutes over a low heat. Then add the lemon juice and check the seasoning. If you want more curry sauce, add some water.

4 When ready to serve, sprinkle with freshly ground black pepper and garam masala powder. Stir well. Put into a serving dish and garnish with the chopped fresh cilantro leaves.

Ideal with boiled Basmati rice.

lamb shank korma (nalli korma) *lucknow*

This Lucknowi recipe is made using only lamb shanks or *nallis* as they are called in India. It has a rich, thick gravy, not particularly spicy but aromatic with cardamom, mace, essence of *keora* or the screwpine flower, and saffron.

The dish has a Moghul influence. Originally almonds would almost certainly have been used instead of cashew nuts, but you can use a mixture of the two, for even better effect.

The flavor and consistency of the marrow-bone stock is essential to this dish. If you wish to use boneless meat, then make a stock with shank bones, 2 cloves garlic, 1 bay leaf and boil for 1 hour. Strain and use instead of water to make the gravy.

Serves 4

a few strands of saffron
1 tablespoon keora *or*
rosewater
1/2 cup oil
2 medium onions, thinly
sliced
1¹/2oz cashew nuts
(or a mixture of almonds
and cashews)
4 green chiles, chopped
2 cinnamon or bay leaves
1 tablespoon chopped ginger
1 tablespoon chopped garlic
2¹/4lb lamb shanks
2 teaspoons coriander
powder
1 teaspoon garam masala
powder
salt
2 teaspoons red chile powder
3 tablespoons full-fat yogurt
³/4 teaspoon mace powder
¹/3 teaspoon cardamom
powder (or 3 green
cardamoms pounded with
a little water)
juice of 1 lime

1 Soak the saffron strands in the *keora* or rosewater for a minimum of 15 minutes.

2 Heat half the oil in a cooking pot and fry the onions until medium-brown. Add the cashew nuts and almonds, if using, and continue to fry until the onions are deep brown.

3 Using a spatula, extract the oil from the onions by pressing them against the side of the pot. Transfer the onions and nuts to a bowl and leave to cool. Place in a blender and purée.

4 In the remaining oil sauté the green chiles, cinnamon or bay leaves, ginger, garlic, lamb, coriander powder, half the garam masala, and 1¹/2 teaspoons of salt for 10 minutes, stirring continuously. Then, over a low heat, add the red chile powder and the yogurt, stir continuously for 3 minutes, and leave to simmer until the yogurt is absorbed.

5 Add the fried onion purée and mix well. Add the remaining garam masala, the mace and cardamom powders, and sauté for a couple of minutes. Add 4 cups of water and cook until the meat is tender. Before transferring to a serving dish, stir in the lime juice and the saffron in the flower water.

Chops or steaks can be used instead of lamb shanks; these are much smaller in India than in the West.

meat curry with cumin-flavored potatoes
(jeera aloo salan) *lucknow*

Salan is the Indian Muslim term for a curry of meat and vegetables cooked together. Meat cooked with potatoes is a popular dish all over Northern India and Pakistan. This recipe is from a gourmet Muslim family in Lucknow.

Serves 4

4 potatoes, a little bigger
  than an egg
salt
1 teaspoon garam masala
  powder
2 teaspoons coriander
  powder
1 teaspoon cumin powder
1 teaspoon red chile powder
  or paprika
1/3 cup oil
3/4 teaspoon cumin seeds
7oz onions, thinly sliced
2 cinnamon or bay leaves
2 large black cardamoms
2 green cardamoms
1/4-in blade of mace
2 teaspoons chopped fresh
  ginger
2 teaspoons chopped garlic
1 1/2lb stewing lamb
  plus a couple of lamb
  bones, chopped
2-in cinnamon stick
6 cloves
7oz tomatoes, finely
  chopped

1 Rub the potatoes with a little salt and set aside for 15 minutes. Rinse and dry. Mix the 4 spice powders with 2 teaspoons of water to make a paste. Reserve.

2 In a cooking pot, heat the oil and cumin seeds. When hot add the potatoes and sauté until golden and crispy. Remove the potatoes and set aside. Strain the cumin seeds from the oil and put 3 tablespoons of the strained oil back into the pot.

3 Add the onions and fry until medium-brown, stirring from time to time. Add the cinnamon or bay leaves, the seeds of the black cardamom, the whole green cardamoms, and the mace. Continue to fry until the onions are deep brown, which will take about 25 minutes in all.

4 Add the spice paste and stir-fry for a minute or two, then add 2 tablespoons of water. Add the ginger and garlic and fry for another 30 seconds.

5 Now put in the lamb and bones with the cinnamon and cloves and sauté for 5–7 minutes, stirring every now and then. Add the tomatoes and let the meat fry in this mixture until the liquid from the tomatoes evaporates.

6 Add 3 1/2 cups of water and 1 1/4 teaspoons salt. Cover and cook over a low heat for 35 minutes. Then put in the fried potatoes and cook until the meat is tender, making sure that the potatoes do not overcook (8–10 minutes). Remove the bones and cinnamon or bay leaves, and add more salt if required. If you want more curry, then add an extra 1/2 cup of water when putting in the potatoes.

lamb in pickling spices (aachar gosht) *bhopal*

Aachar is the Indian word for pickles, which are usually made using mustard oil and a special combination of spices (the same spices that are used in this dish). The curry has its origins in the courtly families of Bhopal, and first made its appearance on a menu in the Haveli restaurant at the Taj Mahal Hotel in Delhi. However, this is a homestyle recipe.

The curry has a sourish tang, is greenish in color and is not as hot as the ingredients would suggest because the chiles mellow down when braised in yogurt. It would traditionally be made using mustard oil. However, this oil has its own strong aroma and is not to everybody's taste, so any other oil may be substituted. Since the green chiles are to be eaten whole, they can be de-seeded to make them milder, if liked.

It can be eaten with a pulao rather than a dry boiled rice, as there is little gravy, or with soft rotis or parathas.

Serves 4

1 1/2 lb stewing lamb plus a
  few bones or a combination
  of 4 lamb chops and
  stewing lamb
9oz plain yogurt
1 tightly packed cup of
  cilantro leaves with stalks
1 1/4 onions, chopped
2 teaspoons chopped garlic
1 1/2 teaspoons chopped
  fresh ginger
1 1/2 teaspoons fennel seeds
1 teaspoon cumin seeds
3/4 teaspoon mustard seeds
1 teaspoon nigella seeds
  (kalonji)
3/4 teaspoon fenugreek seeds
1/4 cup oil
8 long, thin green chiles or
  Spanish chiles
a pinch of turmeric powder
salt

1 Soak the lamb in warm water for 15 minutes to lighten the color. Purée the yogurt and cilantro leaves in a blender: set aside. Purée the onions, garlic, and ginger in the same way.

2 Lightly pound the fennel, cumin, mustard, nigella, and fenugreek seeds in a mortar with a pestle. Slit the chiles down the middle and stuff them with half the spice mixture. Reserve the remaining half.

3 In a shallow cooking pot or deep skillet, heat the oil. Add the chiles and fry until they are pale in color. Add the puréed onion mixture and cook for about 7–10 minutes over a moderate heat until the mixture turns pink in color.

4 Lower the heat, add the reserved spice mixture, and sauté for 1 minute, then put in the yogurt mixture, season with the turmeric powder and 1 teaspoon of salt, stirring continuously to prevent the yogurt from curdling. Bring to a boil, then add the meat (and bones, if used) and mix well. After a minute, turn the heat down very low, cover with a lid, and leave to cook until tender (about 45 minutes). Remove the bones before serving.

lamb with spinach (palak gosht) *punjab*

Punjab is home to an earthy cuisine. The fields are full of wheat, rice, corn, mustard, tomatoes and other wonderful vegetables which the people cook well and almost always douse with home-made butter. And they love their chicken and mutton too!

This is a homestyle dish, also often found in restaurants, and is best eaten with parathas or rotis.

Serves 4

1 1/2lb lamb
3/4 x 1/2-in piece of
  fresh ginger
2 plump cloves garlic
1–2 green chiles
1/2 cup plain yogurt
1/4 teaspoon cumin powder
7oz spinach leaves or
  frozen puréed spinach
1/4 cup oil
1 cinnamon or bay leaf
1 black cardamom
2 cloves
1 large onion, chopped
1 teaspoon coriander powder
1/2 teaspoon cumin powder
2 medium tomatoes,
  chopped
1 tablespoon tomato paste
1 teaspoon salt
little nutmeg powder
a knob of butter (optional)

1 Soak the lamb in warm water for 15 minutes to lighten the color.

2 Purée the ginger, garlic, and green chile in a blender. Whisk the yogurt and add to the ginger/garlic purée, together with the cumin powder.

3 Marinate the lamb in this mixture for at least 1 hour, longer if possible. Meanwhile, blanch the spinach in boiling water with a little salt for 10 seconds, then drain and purée the spinach.

4 Heat the oil in a cooking pot with the cinnamon or bay leaf, cardamom, and cloves. When the oil is really hot and the cinnamon leaf begins to fry, add the onions. Fry for 15 minutes over a low to moderate heat.

5 Add the coriander powder and sauté for 2 minutes, stirring continuously. Add the 1/2 teaspoon of cumin powder and after 10 seconds add a little water. Allow the spices to cook.

6 Add the meat and its marinade, stir well, and cook over a moderate heat for 10 minutes, until the yogurt is absorbed. Sauté the meat for 3 minutes, stirring continuously, then add the tomatoes and tomato paste, and cook for a couple of minutes. Add 1 1/4 cups of hot water and 3/4 teaspoon of the salt. Turn the heat to low, cover with a lid, and leave to simmer. When the meat is almost done, add the puréed spinach, taste for salt, and mix well. Cook for 5 minutes, uncovered. When ready to serve, sprinkle with a little nutmeg powder, and add a knob of butter if you like.

meat cooked with cardamom (elaichi gosht)
sindhi, from mumbai

The Hindu Sindhis migrated from Sindh to India in 1947 (Sindh is now part of Pakistan) and the largest number of them settled in Bombay, now known as Mumbai. Sindhi food is not found outside Sindhi homes. This is my mother's recipe and is extremely simple to make, involving just a few ingredients.

A very delicate mutton dish with a thin gravy full of the flavor of cardamom *(elaichi)* and black pepper, this is a favorite of the Sindhis. Dishes with pepper seem to be a standard prescription in many parts of India for women after childbirth, and in the region around Hyderabad town in Sindh this dish was given every day to new mothers. It is traditionally eaten with chapatis though it is equally good with rice.

Serves 6

2¼lb lamb, on or off
   the bone
½ cup plain yogurt
35 green cardamoms
½ cup oil
2 teaspoons ground black
   pepper
1 teaspoon turmeric powder
1 teaspoon chile powder
2 teaspoons coriander
   powder
3 medium tomatoes (sourish
   variety), finely chopped
salt

1 If the lamb is on the bone, wash it in warm water. Whisk the yogurt with a fork in a bowl.

2 Grind the whole green cardamoms in a blender with a little water, or in a coffee grinder without water and then mix with a little water to make a paste.

3 Heat the oil in a cooking pot. Add the cardamom paste and the pepper, and fry over a low heat for 2–3 minutes. Add the meat and the turmeric, chile, and coriander powders, and sauté for 10 minutes, stirring all the time to prevent the mixture from sticking to the bottom of the pot, adding water if necessary.

4 Lower the heat and add the yogurt, tomatoes, and salt to taste, and continue to sauté for a further 5 minutes. Add about 4 cups of water, cover the pot, and leave to simmer over a low heat until the meat is tender.

The secret of success with this dish lies in making sure that the meat and spices are fried for a full 10 minutes (step 3) without allowing the spices to burn. Therefore it is essential to keep the heat low and use the recommended amount of oil.

lamb slow-cooked in onions and yogurt
(seyal gosht) *sindhi, from mumbai*

Seyal in the Sindhi language means cooking in onions and herbs without adding any water. Lamb (or, in India, mutton) is braised in lots of chopped onions, tomato and yogurt and flavored with whole and ground spices and herbs. It has a wholesome taste and makes a nice family dish. The curry has a thick-textured gravy.

It is eaten with rotis or may be heaped on slices of bread because of the thick onion gravy: perfect this way for a brunch, Sunday lunch or high tea. If you want to eat it with rice, then make a pulao.

Serves 6

4 large onions, chopped
3 small tomatoes
1 1/2 cups plain yogurt
2 cups cilantro leaves
3 green chiles
2 1/4 lb mixture of stewing lamb
  and lamb chops
4 cinnamon or bay leaves
2 large black cardamoms
6 green cardamoms
1 blade of mace
2-in cinnamon stick
12 peppercorns
6 cloves
2/3 cup oil
6 teaspoons chopped ginger
6 teaspoons chopped garlic
4 1/2 teaspoons coriander
  powder
2 teaspoons cumin powder
1/2 teaspoon turmeric powder
2 teaspoons red chile powder
  (or paprika for a milder
  result)
1 teaspoon caraway seeds
1 teaspoon green cardamom
  powder

1 Purée the onions in a blender and place in a bowl. In the same blender purée the tomatoes and transfer to another bowl.

2 Again in the blender, purée the yogurt, coriander leaves, and green chiles. Marinate the lamb in this mixture for at least 1 hour.

3 Make a *bouquet garni* by tying up the cinnamon or bay leaves, black and green cardamoms, mace, cinnamon, peppercorns, and cloves in a small piece of muslin. (In India the spices are put directly into the cooking pot and you can do this if you do not mind avoiding them while eating.)

4 Heat half the oil in a cooking pot, then add the onion purée and cook over a moderate heat for 20 minutes so that some of the moisture evaporates. Stir from time to time.

5 Meanwhile, put the remaining oil with the *bouquet garni* or whole spices in a skillet over a low heat. After 2 minutes add the ginger and garlic, followed 2 minutes later by the coriander, cumin, turmeric, and red chile powders together with 3 tablespoons of water. Stir well to blend with the oil. Sauté for 2 minutes, then pour into the onion mixture.

6 Add the puréed tomato and sauté for about 5 minutes. Leave to cool, then add the meat and yogurt and marinate for 1 further hour.

7 Add 2 teaspoons of salt and mix well. Cook over a high heat for 5 minutes so that the meat juices are sealed. Now reduce the heat to low and gently cook until the meat is tender; or you can transfer it to an earthenware dish and cook in an oven pre-heated to 325°F for 1 1/2 hours. Before serving, discard the bouquet garni, if using, pound the caraway seeds and sprinkle them over with the cardamom powder for a wonderful aroma.

lamb with apricots (jardaloo boti) *mumbai*

Lamb or chicken with apricots is a popular Parsee dish, and the Persian influence shows because it is the Hunza or Afghani apricots that are used. These are the best ones to use but those found in supermarkets can be substituted.

This is quite a simple dish to prepare, and has a tinge of sweet and sour. It is best with a yellow-colored rice but can also be eaten just with side vegetables, as in Western cuisine.

Serves 4

4oz dried Hunza apricots
$1/4$ cup oil
2 medium onions, very finely
  chopped
$1/2$-in square piece of fresh
  ginger, chopped
2 plump cloves garlic,
  finely chopped
3-in cinnamon stick
6 green cardamoms
$1^1/2$ teaspoons red chile
  powder
$1/2$ teaspoon cumin powder
2 tomatoes, chopped
$1^1/2$lb stewing lamb
$3/4$ teaspoon garam masala
  powder
$1/4$ teaspoon ground black
  pepper
salt
1 teaspoon plus a few drops
  of wine vinegar
1 teaspoon sugar

1 Soak the apricots in 1 cup of water with $1/2$ teaspoon of vinegar, for 3 hours. Remove the stones.

2 Heat the oil in a cooking pot and fry the onions for about 12 minutes until golden-brown. Add the ginger and garlic. After 3 minutes, add the cinnamon and cardamoms. After a further minute, add the chile and cumin powders, and stir well.

3 Add the tomatoes and cook for 5 minutes. Then add the meat, garam masala powder, and pepper and stir-fry in the spices for about 5 minutes. Add salt to taste, together with 1 cup of water, then cook slowly over a very low heat until tender. If all the liquid evaporates, add a further $1/2$ cup of water.

4 When the meat is done, add 1 teaspoon of vinegar, the sugar, and the drained apricots, and cook for a further 10 minutes, mixing well. Serve.

bori curry (kaari) *mumbai*

The Boris are a Muslim trading community originally from Gujarat but now living only in Mumbai and a few places in Gujarat. Their cuisine is well liked by the people of Mumbai and certain dishes, like biryani and *khichda* (a wheat, meat and lentil porridge) are relished by everyone. This curry is not well known as it is not available in restaurants. It is called a *kaari* and the Aga Khanis, also a Muslim community, call it a Curry Chawal (*chawal* meaning rice). They buy a ready-mixed curry powder from their grocers that contains the powdered peanuts and grams (*chanas*). This recipe enables you to make this curry without resorting to the commercial powder and blends the Moghul richness of nuts with the flavors of Mumbai—coconut, sesame seeds and curry leaves.

Serves 4

10 almonds, 8 cashew nuts
1 tablespoon roasted peanuts
1 tablespoon roasted gram
2 teaspoons sesame seeds
1 onion, chopped
4 heaped teaspoons
  coriander seeds
2 teaspoons cumin seeds
12 dried whole red chiles
6 teaspoons dried coconut
2/3 cup fresh coconut, sliced
1oz tamarind pulp
9oz medium potatoes
1/3 cup oil
5 cloves
6-in cinnamon stick
6 peppercorns
15 curry leaves
salt
1 1/4 small onions, sliced
1 1/2lb stewing lamb and a
  few bones for stock
1/2 teaspoon turmeric powder
1/2 teaspoon garam masala
3 green chiles
1/2 cup cilantro leaves
1 tablespoon mint leaves

1 To prepare the spice mixture, put the almonds, cashew nuts, peanuts, gram, sesame seeds, and the onion in a pan or on a griddle, and heat for about 5 minutes. Remove and set aside. Now put in the coriander seeds, cumin seeds, dried red chiles, and dried coconut, and heat for just 2 minutes (the griddle will be hot already). Put all the nuts and spices into a blender, add 1/2 cup of water, and grind to a paste.

2 Cut the fresh coconut into pieces. Put into a blender with 2 cups of water and liquidize. Strain the liquid and set aside.

3 Soak the tamarind pulp in 1/2 cup of water. Peel the potatoes and cut into half crossways, or if using large potatoes, cut into quarters.

4 Heat the oil in a cooking pot and when hot add the cloves, cinnamon, peppercorns, and half the curry leaves, and fry over a low heat for 2 minutes. Add the potatoes and a little salt and fry for 5 minutes. Remove the potatoes and set aside.

5 Add the sliced onions to the pot and fry for 7–8 minutes. Add the meat and fry for 5 minutes, then add the remaining curry leaves, 3 cups of water, and salt to taste, and cook for about 40 minutes over a low heat.

6 Add the nut and spice paste, the turmeric and garam masala powders, and the green chiles. Add the tamarind water and stir.

7 Add the potatoes, coconut milk, cilantro leaves, and mint leaves and cook covered for 30 minutes or until the meat is tender. Remove from the heat and keep covered until ready to serve.

Besan flour is made from roasted gram flour, so if grams are difficult to get, you should be able to buy besan from an Indian grocer. Put a tablespoon of besan flour into the spice mixture when grinding, instead of roasted grams.

mutton curry (andhra style) *nellore in andhra*

In India, mutton refers to goat meat, but this curry can be made with lamb. Andhra cuisine is the spiciest and hottest cuisine in India, and the chile powder used is the hottest variety—from Guntur. However, the cooling quality of the yogurt balances the heat of the chile powder in this recipe, which is from the home of Mr Chenna Reddy, a former Chief Minister of Andhra, who keeps an excellent table. Mrs Reddy supervises all the cooking, and this is her recipe. I have reduced the garlic and ginger by half a teaspoon each, as the full quantity can be overpowering for some.

This curry should be eaten with rice, or if made a little thicker by adding less water, is equally delicious with rotis.

Serves 4

$^1/_2$ cup plain yogurt
$2^1/_2$ teaspoons garlic purée
$2^1/_2$ teaspoons ginger purée
2 teaspoons red chile powder
$^1/_2$ teaspoon turmeric powder
2 tablespoons chopped
   cilantro leaves
$1^1/_2$lb stewing lamb
3 tablespoons oil
2 medium onions, finely
   chopped
6 green cardamoms
4 cloves
3 medium tomatoes, finely
   chopped
$^1/_2$ teaspoon caraway seeds
10–12 curry leaves
salt

1 Whisk the yogurt well and add the garlic and ginger purée, the chile and turmeric powders, and the cilantro leaves. Mix well. Marinate the meat in this mixture for 2–4 hours. If it is warm, then put the meat into the refrigerator.

2 Heat the oil in a cooking pot and fry the onions until medium-brown. Add the cardamoms and cloves and fry for 1 minute.

3 Add the meat with the marinade and after 5 minutes turn the heat to very low. Cook for about 10 minutes until the marinade is absorbed. Then sauté or *bhuna* the meat (see step 7 on page 70), stirring continuously for about 5 minutes.

4 Now add the tomatoes and cook for 5 minutes until the liquid is absorbed. Then *bhuna* again for 5 minutes.

5 Add the caraway seeds, curry leaves, and salt to taste, and stir for 2 minutes. Then add 3-4 cups of hot water (depending on the consistency of gravy required) and leave to cook, covered, over a low heat, until the meat is tender.

You can add potatoes to this curry if you wish, in which case, peel and cut 2 medium-sized potatoes into quarters (or use 6–8 small potatoes) and put into the mixture 20 minutes before it is ready. Increase the water added by $^3/_4$ cup and add an extra pinch of salt.

lamb with plums (gosht alu bakhara) *punjab*

This is one of the most interesting curry dishes that I have encountered. It is a speciality of the Veeraswamy restaurant in Piccadilly, London, which is the oldest Indian restaurant in the world. The dish is Hyderabadi in origin, as was the founder of Veeraswamy, Edward Palmer, whose grandmother was a Hyderabadi princess.

Serves 4

4 tablespoons oil

2 medium onions, chopped

4 cloves garlic, chopped

1 x ½-in piece of fresh
  ginger, peeled and chopped

3 cloves

4 green cardamoms

1-in cinnamon stick

3 green chiles, finely
  chopped

¼ teaspoon turmeric powder

1½ teaspoons coriander
  powder

2 teaspoons red chile powder

1½lb boneless stewing lamb

1 teaspoon salt

1½ cups plums with skin
  (half finely chopped and
  half cut into wedges)

3 tablespoons cilantro
  leaves, chopped

8fl oz stock of lamb
  bones if possible (use plain
  water if not)

1 In a deep skillet, heat the oil and fry the onions until they are golden and starting to brown at the edges (this should take about 10–15 minutes). Add the garlic, ginger, cloves, cardamoms, cinnamon, and green chiles. After 1 minute, add the turmeric, coriander, and chile powders. Stir well.

2 Add the lamb and salt and stir-fry in the spice mixture for 5 minutes. Then cover and cook the lamb in its own moisture with the onions on a medium heat for about 10 minutes. When the lamb is semi-dry, stir continuously until it is coated with the spices and the mixture is golden brown.

3 Now add the finely chopped plums and cook with the lamb, stirring a few times. Add 2 tablespoons of the chopped cilantro leaves and the lamb stock or plain water, bring to a boil and simmer over a low heat for 30 minutes. Now add the plum wedges and cook until the lamb is done. Put in a serving dish and sprinkle with the remaining tablespoon of fresh cilantro leaves.

This dish can be eaten with pulao rice or any kind of roti or naan.

meat with lentils (dalcha) *hyderabad*

Cooking lamb or mutton with lentils is popular in northern and western India. The North Indians make *daal gosht*, the Parsees in the West make *dhansak*, the Boris of Mumbai make *khichda* and the Hyderabadi Muslims make *haleem* and *dalcha*. *Dalcha* has a sourish tang with herbal overtones of curry leaves and fresh cilantro.

Serves 8

a few lamb bones
1 bay leaf
1 clove garlic
9oz gram dal (chana dal)
9oz toor dal
2oz tamarind
salt
3/4 teaspoon turmeric powder
6 green chiles, chopped
3 tablespoons cilantro
  leaves, chopped
25 curry leaves
8 tablespoons oil
9oz onions, sliced
6 cloves
6 green cardamoms
4-in cinnamon stick
2 teaspoons red chile powder
3 teaspoons garlic purée
3 teaspoons ginger purée
1 1/2lb stewing lamb
3 tomatoes, chopped

For the seasoning
6 dried red chiles, each
  broken into 2 pieces
  (optional)
3 cloves garlic, crushed
1 teaspoon cumin seeds
1/4 teaspoon mustard seeds
1/3 teaspoon garam masala
  powder

1 Put the lamb bones to boil in 5 cups of water with the bay leaf and garlic clove for 30 minutes. Skim off the scum. Strain the stock and set aside.

2 Wash both dals and soak them separately for 4 hours. Soak the tamarind in 1 cup of water for 1 hour, then press out the juice, strain and set aside the tamarind water.

3 Put both dals into a cooking pot with 8 cups of water and 1 teaspoon of salt, the turmeric powder, 3 of the green chiles, 1 tablespoon of the coriander leaves, and 10 of the curry leaves. Cook for 1 1/2 hours or until tender. Liquidise to a creamy consistency.

4 Heat half the oil in another large cooking pot and sauté the onions for 5–7 minutes. Then add the cloves, cardamoms, cinnamon, the remaining green chiles, the red chile powder, the remaining coriander, and 10 of the curry leaves, and the garlic and ginger purée. Stir to prevent the spices from sticking to the pot. Sprinkle over 2 tablespoons of water if necessary.

5 Add the lamb and sauté over a moderate heat for 5 minutes. Add the tomatoes and sauté for a further 5 minutes. Stir in the puréed dals and the stock, adding more water to total 4 cups. Add salt to taste (about 3/4 teaspoon) and leave to cook, covered, over a moderate heat, until the lamb is tender. This should take about 50–60 minutes. Then add the tamarind water and remaining curry leaves and simmer for a couple of minutes.

6 Just before serving, season by heating the remaining oil in a large ladle or small frying pan and frying the red chiles, if used, the garlic, cumin seeds, mustard seeds, and garam masala powder (in this order). Fry for 10 seconds after the addition of the last ingredient. Add this seasoning to the curry and stir. It is now ready to serve.

lamb curry (madras style) *tamil nadu*

The standard Madras curry in restaurants in the UK is not to be found anywhere in Madras! However, once when I was travelling into the deep south of the Coromandel coast of India, near the seventeenth-century Danish settlement of Tranquebar, it was lunch-time and there was no eatery in sight. The local village cook made a stunning mutton curry, that I have reproduced here using lamb. Easy to make, it is perfect for a get-together with family or friends.

Serves 6

1 cup fresh coconut
3 or 4 whole Guajillo chiles,
    dried, or 3 teaspoons
    cayenne pepper or
    paprika powder
1 x ¹/₂-in piece
    of fresh ginger
6 plump cloves garlic
3 teaspoons paprika powder
3 teaspoons coriander
    powder
4 peppercorns
2 cinnamon or bay leaves
4-in cinnamon stick
6 cloves
1 teaspoon cumin seeds
1 teaspoon poppy seeds
¹/₂ teaspoon fennel seeds
3 tablespoons oil
2 large onions, chopped
2¹/₄lb stewing lamb
3 tomatoes, chopped
salt

1 Cut half the coconut into small pieces for grinding with the spices and set aside. Cut the remainder into pieces and put into a blender with 2 cups of warm water. Blend until smooth, then strain and reserve the coconut milk.

2 Grind together the chopped coconut, chiles, and the ginger, garlic and all the spices to make a smooth paste, adding a little water.

3 Heat the oil in a cooking pot and fry the onions until brown. Add the spice paste and fry for about 15 minutes over a low heat, stirring in 3 tablespoons of water in the process.

4 Add the meat and sauté for 5 minutes over a moderate heat. Add the tomatoes and sauté for a further 5 minutes. Add salt to taste.

5 Add 4 cups of warm water and cook, covered, until the meat is done (about 50–60 minutes). Then add the coconut milk and simmer for a few minutes before serving.

goa lamb vindaloo *goa*

Vindaloo is a dish made by the descendants of, or those who lived in areas dominated by, the Portuguese. It is primarily made with chiles, garam masala, garlic and vinegar. The word vindaloo comes from a combination of *vin* for vinegar and *aloo* from *alho*, which is Portuguese for garlic. The chiles were introduced into Goa by the Portuguese, and the garam masala spices were those traded in the sixteenth and seventeenth centuries.

This is one of the best vindaloo recipes. You can make it as hot as you want. Phil Mendes from Goa, whose recipe it is, likes her food spicy but not searing hot and therefore she de-seeds the red chiles. Vindaloo in Goa was and is traditionally made with pork. It is best with boiled rice.

Serves 4

15–20 whole red chiles
  (preferably Kashmiri type)
  or 3^1/$_2$ teaspoons cayenne
  pepper
1 teaspoon cumin seeds
6 cloves
2-in cinnamon stick
10 peppercorns
^{1}/$_4$ star anise
1 teaspoon poppy seeds
2 x ^{1}/$_4$-in piece of
  fresh ginger
6 plump cloves garlic
1 tablespoon tamarind pulp
4 teaspoons cider vinegar
^{1}/$_3$ cup oil
3 medium onions, finely
  chopped
1^1/$_2$lb stewing lamb, cubed
salt
^{1}/$_2$ teaspoon jaggery, to taste
15 curry leaves

1 Soak the chiles in a little water to soften. Then grind all the spices, ginger, garlic and tamarind with the vinegar to make a smooth paste. Rub a little mixture onto the lamb and marinate for 15 minutes.

2 Heat the oil in a cooking pot and fry the onions for about 15–20 minutes until brown. Add the spice paste and fry for a further 5 minutes, stirring continuously and adding 2 tablespoons of water, if necessary.

3 Add the lamb and sauté in the spice mixture for 5 minutes. Add 4 cups of water, salt to taste, and the jaggery and cook over a low heat until tender. Stir in the curry leaves and simmer for 3–4 minutes; the vindaloo is now ready to serve.

The vinegar and oil in the dish act as preservatives and it freezes extremely well. It can also be kept in the refrigerator for 2 days and will, in fact, be better the day after cooking.

You can also make just the spice paste in large batches and freeze it, using small amounts as and when required.

This dish is equally good using pork or beef.

white chicken korma (safed murgh korma) *agra*

A mild aromatic korma, this is basically a Muslim court dish, a blend of Moghlai and Nawabi cuisine. The Moghul Emperor Shahjehan, builder of the Taj Mahal monument, used to have all-white banquets on full-moon nights at the Agra Fort. The terrace of the fort was bedecked with white carpets and cushions and white flowers, the guests dressed in white, and all the dishes served were white in color. The white korma was later perfected at the tables of the gourmet Nawabs of Oudh in Lucknow. The Royal House of Jaipur, connected by marriage to the Moghuls, also served all-white banquets on the night of Sharad Poornima, the September full moon, as late as the 1960s.

Originally this dish was made with almonds only, but modern cooks prefer a combination of cashews and almonds. The traditional Lucknowi recipe also includes 1oz *chaar magaz* or "four seeds", a mix of various melon, squash and pumpkin seeds available in India from speciality grocers, and a teaspoon of powdered rose petals, but these are omitted here.

Serves 4

1½ teaspoons poppy seeds
5oz plain yogurt
⅓ cup ghee or
   clarified butter
2oz blanched almonds
2oz unsalted cashew nuts
1 cinnamon or bay leaf
2 onions, chopped
3 green chiles, chopped
4 green cardamoms
2 teaspoons finely
   chopped garlic
2 teaspoons finely chopped
   fresh ginger
1 whole green chile
1 clove
2¼lb boneless chicken
   breasts, skinned
½ teaspoon nutmeg powder
½ teaspoon mace powder
salt

1 Soak the poppy seeds in ½ cup of water for 1 hour. Then drain the water and grind into a fine paste.

2 Hang the yogurt in a cheesecloth for 1 hour to drain the whey. Then put the hung yogurt into a bowl and whisk.

3 Heat the ghee or clarified butter in a cooking pot, reserving 1 tablespoon. Then add the almonds, cashews, and cinnamon or bay leaf and fry for about 7–8 minutes over a moderate heat. Add the onions and fry for about 10 minutes or until lightly colored. Add the chopped green chiles, cardamoms, and ground poppy seeds and fry for about 3–4 minutes. Add 1 cup of water and cook for 10 minutes. Remove from the heat, discard the cinnamon or bay leaf and leave to cool. Put the mixture into a blender and purée to a smooth paste without any grains.

4 Add the reserved tablespoon of ghee or clarified butter to the cooking pot, then add the garlic, ginger, whole green chile, and clove. After 1 minute, add the chicken pieces. The chicken will gradually release its juices until the meat is almost dry. Then add the yogurt and stir continuously to prevent it from curdling.

5 Add the ground spice mixture with the nutmeg and mace powders and salt to taste. Stir well and add 1½ cups of hot water. Taste the mixture. If you find it bland, you can add additional whole green chiles. Cook over a low heat until the chicken is tender.

green chicken korma (chicken rizzala) *bhopal*

Rizzala is a little-known Muslim-style curry found in only two cities of India—Calcutta and Bhopal. Its origin is possibly the latter, where it is a curry found only in the homes of the Muslim aristocracy. A fresh herby curry, this can best be described as a green korma.

Serves 4

1/2 cup unroasted cashew
 nuts
6 tablespoons oil
4 medium onions, chopped
2 large handfuls of cilantro
 leaves
1/2 cup mint leaves
4 green chiles
2 bay leaves
6 green cardamoms
1 1/2-in cinnamon stick
1 x 3/4-in piece of fresh
 ginger, peeled and
 finely chopped
4 cloves garlic, chopped
2 1/4lb chicken, skinned and
 cut into 8 pieces
1 heaped teaspoon coriander
 powder
1/2 teaspoon cumin powder
salt to taste
1 teaspoon sugar
2 teaspoons lime or
 lemon juice
2 1/2fl oz cream
1 tablespoon oil, butter or
 ghee
1/4 teaspoon mace powder or
 1 blade of mace

1 Soak the cashew nuts in 1 cup of water, for at least 15 minutes.

2 Pour 4 tablespoons of oil in a skillet and fry the onions over a medium heat until they are crispy brown, but not burnt at the edges. This will take between 20–30 minutes, depending on the thickness of the pan and the heat.

3 When the onions are done, put in a blender with the cilantro leaves, mint leaves, green chiles, soaked cashew nuts, and 1/4 cup of water and purée.

4 In the same pan, heat the remaining 2 tablespoons of oil over a low heat, and add the bay leaves, cardamoms, cinnamon, ginger, and garlic. Then increase the heat to medium, put in the chicken pieces and sauté in the aromatic oil for about 5 minutes until the chicken is seared. Now add the coriander and cumin powder. Sauté the chicken for 2 minutes, stirring so that the chicken doesn't stick to the pan. Add the green purée and sauté the chicken for a further 2 minutes.

5 Add the salt, sugar, and lime juice, and 1 cup of water. Taste and adjust the seasoning. Now bring to a boil and simmer until the chicken is cooked, then add the cream, and stir well.

6 Just before serving, heat a little oil or butter in a ladle and put 1/4 teaspoon of mace powder into ladle. After 10 seconds put it into the pot and stir. Alternatively, if using a blade of mace, remove it from the oil after 20 seconds and just put the oil in. Mix well.

Serve with flavored rice, such as turmeric yellow rice or lemon rice. You could also accompany it with naan bread or chapatis.

butter chicken (murgh makhani) *delhi*

Chicken Makhani, made either with tikkas—derived from the Hindi word *tukra* and meaning pieces—or quarters of chicken, is the most popular dish in Indian restaurants both in India and overseas. It is essentially a restaurant and not a homestyle dish, because there are no tandoors in Indian domestic kitchens, and this dish consists of tandoor-cooked chicken in a sauce.

However, since the dish is so popular, many would like to recreate it at home, and I give a simplified way to do so here, cooking the chicken in a skillet. Alternatively, it is possible to roast a whole small chicken, marinating it first, then quartering it and adding the juices from the roasting pan into the *makhani* sauce.

Butter chicken originated in the 1950s at the Moti Mahal restaurant in Delhi where they made the sauce by adding butter and tomato to the leftover chicken juices in the marinade trays from which they used to sell hundreds of portions of Tandoori Chicken every day.

Serves 4

*2lb chicken, skinned
  quarters, smaller pieces on
  the bone or boneless
  pieces (tikkas)*
4–5 tablespoons oil

For the marinade
2 cups plain yogurt
6 cloves garlic
¹/₂-in square of fresh ginger
*²/₃ teaspoon red chile
  powder or paprika*
*¹/₄ teaspoon coriander
  powder*
¹/₂ teaspoon cumin powder
*¹/₂ teaspoon garam masala
  powder*
*a tiny pinch of tandoori
  coloring (optional)*
¹/₂ teaspoon salt
2 teaspoons lime juice

1 First prepare the marinade. Place the yogurt in a piece of cheesecloth and hang to allow the whey to drip away. Purée the garlic and ginger in a blender. Add this and the marinade spices, salt, and lime juice to the yogurt and mix well.

2 Scald the tomatoes for the *makhani* sauce and peel off the skin. Reduce to a semi-pulp with a fork or potato masher. Put the *kasuri methi* into a grinder and reduce to a powder.

3 Make gashes in the chicken if using pieces on the bone. Marinate the chicken in the yogurt mixture for at least 1 hour, preferably 2; for best results leave overnight.

4 When ready to cook, heat the oil in a large, thick-bottomed skillet and put in the chicken with the marinade. Cover and cook over a low heat until done. Turn the chicken over during cooking.

5 Put the tomato pulp into a skillet and cook for 5 minutes or so until the liquid has evaporated slightly.

6 Add the chilled butter and paprika; after the butter has melted, let it cook for just 1 minute. Taste. If it is not sour, add a few drops of vinegar. Add the *kasuri methi*, garam masala powder, and salt to taste. After 30 seconds, add the cream and stir. The sauce is now ready. Pour it into the skillet and mix well with the chicken. Serve immediately.

For the makhani sauce

1 1/2 lb tomatoes

1/2 teaspoon kasuri methi
   (dried fenugreek leaves)

3oz chilled butter

1/2 teaspoon paprika

few drops of vinegar

1/4 teaspoon garam masala

salt

1 1/2 fl oz light cream

If butter is cooked for as long as 3 minutes it will turn into ghee and become a grainy emulsion. So start with chilled butter and cook for less than 2 minutes after the butter has melted.

You can cook the chicken ahead of time. But makhani sauce takes only 5–6 minutes to prepare and should be made when the dish is to be eaten. You can cook the tomato ahead, but add the butter just before serving.

In India, restaurateurs mix a little raw papaya purée into the marinade as a tenderizer.

chicken pistachio korma (pista chicken) *delhi*

I first ate this dish long ago in a small roadside restaurant in a by-lane in the heart of Mumbai's bazaar areas. Years later I met the cook, who comes from a family of professional wedding caterers near the Jama Masjid mosque area of Old Delhi.

It is very delicate in taste, and attractive to look at with its creamy light green color. The taste depends on the quality of pistachios used—the brighter green, the better. This dish deserves all-white meat, so breast of chicken is best. One can of course make it with a whole chicken as well.

Serves 4

2¹/₄lb chicken
4oz shelled pistachio nuts, unsalted
8 green chiles
5 tablespoons single cream
3 tablespoons plain yogurt
2 onions, chopped
oil
1 x ¹/₂-in piece of fresh ginger, chopped
6 plump cloves garlic
³/₄ teaspoon garam masala powder
¹/₈ teaspoon turmeric powder
2 cinnamon or bay leaves
³/₄ teaspoon ground white pepper
1¹/₄ teaspoons fennel seeds
1 tomato, chopped
salt
1 teaspoon green cardamom powder
2 tablespoons chopped cilantro leaves

1 Cut the chicken into pieces as desired. Use the bones and trimmings to make 3 cups of stock.

2 Boil the pistachios for 10 minutes in 1 cup of water. Remove from the heat, drain and leave to cool. Rub the nuts with your fingers to remove the skin. Grind the pistachios with 4 of the green chiles and cream and reduce to a paste in a blender.

3 Whisk the yogurt well with a fork.

4 Fry the onions in the oil in a cooking pot until lightly colored. Add the ginger, garlic, garam masala and turmeric powders, cinnamon or bay leaves, white pepper, and fennel seeds and fry for 2 minutes. Add the pistachio mixture and fry for 2 minutes.

5 Add the chicken and sauté for 5 minutes. Then add the tomato, yogurt, remaining chiles, and salt to taste. Add the chicken stock (or water) and cook until done, about 15–20 minutes depending on the size of chicken pieces. Sprinkle with cardamom powder and cilantro leaves just before serving.

In India, gourmets use Peshwari pistachios for their taste and bright green color.

chicken and cashew nuts in black spices
(kaju chicken in kaala masala) *mumbai*

Maharashtrians have a powdered spice mixture called *kaala masala* which they use in many dishes. *Kaala* means black, and it is a combination of dark-colored spices, a kind of garam masala with the addition of coriander seeds and cumin.

This is a thick, nutty curry of chicken with lots of cashew nuts, whole and crushed, and is delicious. The recipe comes from the wife of the famous gynaecologist of Mumbai, the late Dr Shirodkar. Eat it with rotis. Lemon rice also goes well with it since the dish has no touch of sourness.

Serves 4

2¹/₄lb chicken, skinned
4oz grated coconut
12 plump cloves
 garlic, peeled
1 x ¹/₂-in piece of fresh
 ginger, chopped
2¹/₂ tablespoons coriander
 seeds
1¹/₂ teaspoons cumin seeds
4 whole dried red chiles
6 cloves
3-in cinnamon stick
8oz cashew nuts
1 large onion, chopped
5 tablespoons oil
salt

1 Cut the chicken into 8 pieces.

2 In a large frying pan, without any fat or oil, roast the coconut, garlic, ginger, coriander seeds, cumin seeds, red chiles, cloves, and cinnamon over a low heat. After 5 minutes, add 2oz of the cashew nuts plus the onion and roast for a further 10 minutes, stirring all the time. Turn off the heat and leave to cool. Grind the mixture in a blender or food-processor with ³/₄ cup of water to a fine consistency.

3 Separately grind 1oz of the remaining cashew nuts with a little water to make a fine paste and set aside.

4 Heat the oil in a cooking pot, add the ground spice mixture, and fry for 10 minutes over a low heat. Add the ground cashew nuts and salt to taste and fry for a further 2–3 minutes.

5 Add the chicken, turn up the heat to moderate, and fry for 5 minutes. Then add 3 cups of water, cover, and leave to cook over a low heat for 10 minutes.

6 Add the remaining cashew nuts and continue to cook until the chicken is done. You should have a thick, dark curry with whole cashew nuts in it.

When grinding the spices and cashew nuts make sure that the resulting paste is smooth and fine by grinding for a long time until you get this consistency. If not, the curry will look as if it has curdled.

chicken cooked with lentils and vegetables (dhansak) *mumbai*

Dhansak is the best-known and liked dish in Parsee cuisine. The Parsees fled Persia to avoid religious persecution in the eighth century and settled on the western coast of India, in what is now Gujarat State. They adopted Gujarati as their language and absorbed local influences into their cuisine. *Dhan* in Gujarati means wealth, but in Parsee Gujarati *Dhaan* means rice. *Sak* means vegetables. Dhansak is a meat, vegetable and lentil curry eaten with a caramelized brown pulao rice. It is often eaten at Sunday lunch but is not served on auspicious occasions since it is customarily eaten on the fourth day after a funeral.

Although there are many ingredients, it is quite simple to prepare. The *dhansak masala* may be available in some Indian grocers, but Parsee *sambar masala* has not yet found its way to the West.

Serves 6

3lb chicken, cut into
  6 or more pieces
10oz toor dal (whole dried
  variety)
2oz tamarind pulp
2-in piece of fresh ginger
6 cloves garlic
2 large onions, chopped
7oz red pumpkin, chopped
5oz eggplant, chopped
1 potato, chopped
1/4 cup fresh dill, chopped
1/2 teaspoon turmeric powder
1 cup plus 1 tablespoon
  cilantro leaves
20 leaves fresh mint
salt
3 1/2fl oz oil
1/2 bunch fresh fenugreek or
  2 teaspoons dried fenugreek
  leaves (kasuri methi)
3 teaspoons Parsee sambar
  masala

1 Make a chicken stock with the bones, neck, giblets, and trimmings.

2 Wash the toor dal and soak it in water for 30 minutes. Soak the tamarind in 1 cup of water for at least 30 minutes.

3 Chop 1 1/2-in piece of the ginger and 4 of the garlic cloves.

4 In a large cooking pot, put the dal to cook in 3 cups of water along with the onions, pumpkin, eggplant, potato, and dill. Add the turmeric, the whole remaining piece of ginger, the remaining 2 garlic cloves, 1 tablespoon of the cilantro leaves, and 8 of the mint leaves. Simmer until the dal is very soft. Allow to cool slightly. Liquidize with an egg-beater to achieve a creamy consistency. Season with 1 teaspoon of salt.

5 While the dal is cooking, heat the oil in a large skillet and add the chopped ginger and garlic, the cup of cilantro, the remaining mint leaves, plus the fenugreek, *sambar masala*, *dhansak masala*, cumin, coriander, and red chile powders, tomatoes, and green chiles, and fry for 2 minutes, stirring continuously. Add the chicken and sauté for 2 minutes. Season with 1 teaspoon of salt and stir well.

6 Add the chicken to the dal along with 3 cups of chicken stock or water. Add the jaggery. Simmer until the chicken is cooked through before adding the tamarind water and lime juice; adjust the salt, then simmer for a couple of minutes. It is now ready to serve.

2 teaspoons **dhansak masala**
1 teaspoon **cumin powder**
3 teaspoons **coriander powder**
2 teaspoons **red chile powder**
3 **tomatoes, chopped**
6 **green chiles, chopped**
1 tablespoon **jaggery or palm sugar**
juice of 1 lime

This is a straightforward and tasty recipe for dhansak. *Parsees who are fastidious use a mix of dals—7oz of toor dal and 1 tablespoon each of moong, masoor and val dal.*

Dhansak *powder in packet form is available at Indian grocers. If unavailable use 1¹/₂ teaspoons of garam masala, ¹/₂ teaspoon of star anise powder, and ¹/₄ teaspoon of nutmeg powder.*

Instead of Parsee sambar masala *make the following mix: ³/₄ teaspoon of fenugreek powder, ¹/₂ teaspoon of mustard powder, 1 teaspoon of red chile powder, and ¹/₂ teaspoon of ground pepper.*

chicken in thick coconut gravy
(kori gashi) *mangalore*

Mangalore is a port town just off Goa on the west coast of India. The cuisine of Mangalore features a lot of seafood and also includes chicken, unlike Goa where chicken is rarely eaten. The gashi is a thick coconut gravy with a grainy texture and this recipe is from a Hindu family. It is reddish-brown in color and slightly on the hot side. The exact degree of spiciness depends on the variety of chile used. In Mangalore the bedgi chile is used, which looks like the Kashmiri chile but is more pungent—with lots of color. This curry is different from other coconut and chile-based curries in that the coconut and spices are fried in oil before grinding, and there are a few unusual spices for this kind of curry—mustard seeds and fenugreek seeds. The tamarind is also ground with the spices. The fresh curry leaves give Kori Gashi a distinctive aroma.

Serves 4–5

2 cups grated coconut
5 tablespoons oil
15 whole dried red chiles
4 heaped teaspoons
   coriander seeds
$^1/_4$ teaspoon mustard seeds
$^1/_2$ teaspoon fenugreek seeds
2-in cinnamon stick
1 teaspoon cumin seeds
8 peppercorns
4 cloves
$^1/_2$ teaspoon turmeric powder
2 teaspoons tamarind pulp
2 cups chopped onion
1 x $^1/_2$-in piece of fresh
   ginger, peeled and chopped
5 plump cloves garlic,
   chopped
2$^1/_4$lb chicken pieces, on or
   off the bone, skinned
salt
10–12 curry leaves

1 Soak half of the grated coconut in 1 cup of warm water for 30 minutes, then put it into a blender to obtain the first extract of milk. Strain and reserve. Then put the coconut and 2 cups of warm water into a blender and blend. Drain the second extract.

2 In a skillet, over a low heat, put 1 tablespoon of the oil just to grease the pan and sauté the remaining coconut for 5 minutes. Remove from heat and set aside.

3 Add another tablespoon of oil just to grease the pan and sauté the red chiles for 2–3 minutes, then add the coriander, mustard and fenugreek seeds, the cinnamon, cumin seeds, peppercorns, cloves, and turmeric, in this order. Stir continuously. One minute after putting in the last item, remove from the heat.

4 Put these spices into a blender with the fried coconut, the tamarind, half the onion, the ginger and garlic, and $^1/_2$ cup of the second coconut milk and blend to make a smooth paste. This will take at least 5 minutes.

5 Heat 3 tablespoons of the oil in a cooking pot. Sauté the remaining chopped onion until medium-brown; this will take about 15 minutes.

6 Add the spice paste together with a little water and sauté for 3 minutes, then add the chicken and sauté for a few minutes. After 5 minutes, add the remaining second extract of coconut milk and salt to taste. Add 1 cup of water. Cook over a low heat, covered, until the chicken is almost done, then add the first extract of coconut milk and the curry leaves, and boil for just 1 minute.

chicken chettinad (kozhi varatha kosambu)
chettinad

Chettinad is the region in southern Tamil from where the Chettiars, the trader and mercantile community of the region, originate. They have traded with south-east Asia for over a thousand years. In 1077AD the Chola King Kulottunga sent an embassy of 72 merchants to the Chinese court. One can see this influence in the use of star anise, a popular spice in Chinese cooking, in these curries. Chettinad cuisine is presently the rage in Madras: the first Chettinad restaurant, "The Raintree," opened in the mid-1980s, and has been followed by several others.

Chettinad cuisine is hot. The chicken is always cut in very small pieces on the bone—about 12 pieces from a chicken. This is an ideal dish to make using chicken drumsticks. Since it is dryish, this reddish-brown dish can be eaten with a flavored rice like lemon or tomato rice.

Serves 5

2 teaspoons poppy seeds
1/2lb fresh coconut
1 teaspoon fennel seeds
2-in cinnamon stick
3 green cardamoms
4 cloves
3/4 teaspoon turmeric powder
3/4 teaspoon garam masala
  powder
1/3 cup oil
1 large onion, chopped
2 teaspoons fresh ginger,
  finely chopped
2 teaspoons garlic, chopped
1/2 star anise
3 teaspoons red chile powder
2 1/2lb chicken, cut as
  preferred
3 medium tomatoes,
  chopped
salt
juice of 1/2 lime
a few curry leaves
1/3 cup cilantro leaves,
  chopped

1 On a griddle or in a crêpe pan, toast the poppy seeds for a few minutes until light brown. Crush with a rolling pin, then soak in a little water for 15 minutes.

2 Grind the coconut together with the poppy and fennel seeds, cinnamon, cardamom, cloves, turmeric, and garam masala to make a fine paste.

3 Heat the oil in a large shallow cooking pot and sauté the onion until lightly colored. Add the ginger and garlic, then 2 minutes later add the star anise and red chile powder, followed by the spice paste. Sauté for 5 minutes, adding a little more water if required.

4 Add the chicken and sauté for 5 minutes. Add the tomatoes. When the chicken has absorbed the tomato juice, add 2 cups of water and salt to taste and mix well. When almost done, add the lime juice and curry leaves. Just before serving, sprinkle with the cilantro leaves.

chicken stew *kerala*

The word "stew" has become part of the Indian culinary vocabulary. In Southern India, stew is made with coconut milk and Malabar coast spices. In Kerala in particular it is commonly eaten with *appams* or rice flour pancakes for breakfast or Sunday brunch. In northern India, even roadside eateries serve a mild curry which they can stew.

The dish can be made milder still by reducing the green chile, but it is really aromatic. A lady from Kerala says that she thinks the combination of ghee and oil imparts a special flavor. The Keralites use very tiny pieces of chicken on the bone, but you can use small boneless pieces, if you like. On the bone, this quantity will serve 4, but boneless should be enough for 5 people.

Serves 4–5

1 x ¾-in piece of fresh
  ginger (half cut into thin
  julienne, half cut into
  pieces)
1 teaspoon peppercorns
a little turmeric powder
2 onions, coarsely chopped
2–3 green chiles
2 cups grated fresh coconut
10–12 new potatoes
salt, to taste
2 tablespoons oil
1 tablespoon ghee
½ teaspoon mustard seeds
1 cinnamon or bay leaf
2 cloves garlic, sliced
  lengthwise
2-in cinnamon stick
4 cardamoms
3 cloves
20 curry leaves
1¾lb boneless, skinless
  chicken pieces
1 carrot, peeled and cut into
  ¾-in strips
½ cup fresh or frozen peas
¼ teaspoon garam masala

1 Pound the ginger pieces (retain the julienne strips for later), peppercorns, and a little turmeric and make into a thick, uneven paste.

2 Blend together the onion and green chiles. Put the grated coconut into 2 cups of water and blend to make an extract of milk. Strain and keep to one side.

3 Scrub the potatoes and half-boil them in their skin with a pinch of salt and turmeric.

4 Heat the oil and ghee, and when hot, add the mustard seeds. When the seeds crackle, add the cinnamon or bay leaf. When the mixture turns a khaki color add the garlic, cinnamon stick, and cardamoms. After 20 seconds, add the ginger and turmeric paste, cloves, and curry leaves, then add the onion and green chiles. After 2 minutes put in the chicken pieces and sauté for 2–3 minutes.

5 Add the potatoes, carrot, and salt to taste and cook, covered, for 2 minutes. Finally add the coconut milk, ½ cup of water, the peas, and juliennes of ginger. Sprinkle with garam masala powder, cover, and cook until the chicken is cooked.

chicken dopiaza (chicken with onions) *bengal*

Dopiaza is a popular dish in Indian restaurants outside India. *Do* means two and *piaz* means onions in Hindi, and the term describes a dish using twice the normal proportion of onions, or in which onions are used twice in the cooking process. Dopiaza is essentially an Indian Muslim dish and Bengal has a tradition of fine Muslim cooking. The province was ruled by the Nawab of Murshidabad and Muslim Moghal governors until the British took over, and the exiled Nawabs of Oudh, as well as the family of Tipu Sultan, came to Calcutta after ceding their kingdom in the south to the British. So there has been an inflow of Muslim culinary influences.

Bengal is a region where people are particular about their food and many Bengali men cook superbly. This is Batuk Bhattacherya's recipe and is the finest dopiaza I have ever tasted. At home Bhattacherya cooks the chicken dishes and his wife makes all the fish ones.

Serves 4

2¹/₂lb small roasting chicken
9 medium onions
8 small potatoes (optional)
3 teaspoons red chile powder
¹/₂ cup plain yogurt
¹/₂ cup oil
2 plump cloves garlic,
 finely chopped
2 cinnamon or bay leaves
2-in cinnamon stick
6 cardamoms
1¹/₂ teaspoons peppercorns
12 cloves
2 whole red chiles
2 tablespoons ginger purée
¹/₂ teaspoon turmeric
2 tomatoes, chopped
1 tablespoon butter
³/₄ teaspoon sugar
salt
1¹/₂ teaspoons garam
 masala powder

1 Cut the chicken into 8 pieces on the bone. Cut 3 of the onions in half. Chop 2 of the onions coarsely. Extract the juice from the remaining 4 onions by grating them and squeezing out the juice through a cheesecloth, discarding the pulp.

2 Peel the potatoes, if using. Mix the chile powder to a paste with a little water. Whisk the yogurt.

3 Heat the oil in a heavy pan and fry the 2 chopped onions until light brown. Remove and drain on kitchen paper, and set aside. In the same oil, fry the garlic, bay leaves and, after a couple of minutes, add the cinnamon and cardamoms. Then, 2 minutes later, add the peppercorns, cloves, and whole red chiles.

4 After 30 seconds, add the ginger purée, chile paste, and turmeric and stir continuously. Add the chicken, potatoes, and tomatoes, followed by the butter, yogurt, and sugar. Cook for 10–12 minutes, stirring so that the spices do not stick to the bottom of the pan, and add a little water, if necessary.

5 Now add the onion halves, followed by the onion juice and salt to taste. Stir for 2–3 minutes. Then transfer to a baking dish and cook in the oven, preheated to 325°F, for 20–25 minutes. When the chicken and potatoes are done, add half the fried onions and sprinkle over the garam masala powder. Sprinkle over the remaining fried onions just before serving.

parsee red chicken curry *mumbai*

I mentioned in the introduction to this book how as a child, I was enamoured by a young Parsee girl sitting next to me eating a bright red chicken curry. I recently asked a Parsee school friend to cook this for me and she told me that it was a popular Parsee homestyle curry. Parsees have traditionally kept Goan cooks at home and so there is also a Goan influence on this curry.

The secret of the red color is to use good-quality dried Kashmiri-style chiles, which are not always available outside of western India. So if you can't get hold of them, use bright red fresh chiles instead. If you don't want the curry very hot, use 5 chiles with their seeds, and the rest without. Some Parsees also add white sesame seeds (1 teaspoon) to the curry mixture — it adds taste but it is not easy to grind fine in some mixers. This curry looks and tastes good and is easy to make. It's best to eat with boiled rice.

Serves 4

10–12 Kashmiri chiles
$3/4$ x $1/2$-in piece of fresh
  ginger, peeled and chopped
2 medium onions, coarsely
  chopped
3 medium tomatoes, chopped
$1/2$ teaspoon cumin seeds
1 teaspoon coriander seeds
1-in piece cassia bark
  or cinnamon stick
1 teaspoon turmeric
8–9 cloves garlic
$1/3$ cup oil
3–4 bay leaves
2lb chicken, cut into
  pieces, as you like
  (preferably with bone)
salt

1 Soak the Kashmiri chiles in a little warm water for about 20 minutes to soften and bloat.

2 Put the Kashmiri chiles, ginger, onions, tomatoes, cumin, coriander seeds, cinnamon, turmeric, and garlic and into a food-processor and blend to a smooth paste.

3 Put the oil in a pan to heat. Add the bay leaves and gently fry for 1 minute. Then add the paste and stir it for 3 minutes.

4 Add the chicken pieces and stir for a further 2 minutes. Add 1 cup water (add more if you prefer a thinner gravy) and salt to taste, cover with a lid and cook on a very slow heat until it's done.

shrimps in sweet and hot curry (shrimp patia)
dahanu, near mumbai

The Parsees fled Persia about 1300 years ago and settled on the coast of Gujarat in India. Others who in recent centuries gradually arrived from Persia formed a small but distinct community in Bombay and Dahanu, just to the north, where they are known as Iranis and cultivate fruit orchards of mangoes, chicoos *(sapotas,)* and lychees. This *patia* recipe is an Irani one from Dahanu. The Parsees also have a version of *patia*.

A *patia* is a curry with sweet, hot, and sour flavors equally balanced. Both Parsees and Iranis serve the *patia* on auspicious family occasions, along with yellow rice and lentils, calling it by its traditional name—*dhan, dar,* or *patio*. The Irani *patia* is slightly spicier and hotter than the Parsee one. There are many chiles in this recipe but the heat is offset by the sour tamarind and the sugar. It is traditionally served with yellow rice.

Serves 2

1lb shelled, uncooked
  shrimp
1 1/2 teaspoons tamarind pulp
5 green chiles, chopped
  (serrano)
3 plump cloves garlic
1 teaspoon cumin seeds
1/4 cup oil
2 large onions, finely
  chopped
1/2 teaspoon cumin powder
3/4 teaspoon coriander
  powder
3/4 teaspoon red chile
  powder
1 teaspoon garam masala
  powder
1/2 teaspoon turmeric powder
2 medium tomatoes, finely
  chopped
1 teaspoon jaggery
10 curry leaves
1/4 cup cilantro leaves
salt

1 If using fresh shrimp, wash and remove the veins.

2 Soak the tamarind in 1/2 cup of warm water for at least 30 minutes.

3 Grind the green chiles, 2 of the garlic cloves, and the cumin seeds to a paste.

4 Heat the oil in a cooking pot and fry the onions until deep pink. Add the ground paste and fry for 2 minutes, stirring well.

5 Add the cumin, coriander, red chile, garam masala, and turmeric powders. Stir constantly for 1 minute. Add the chopped tomatoes and fry for 4–5 minutes, stirring from time to time.

6 Add half the tamarind water, the jaggery, curry and cilantro leaves, and about 1 1/2 teaspoons of salt. Taste and adjust the sour, sweet, and salt flavors to your liking. Add 3/4 cup of water and bring to the boil. Simmer for 5 minutes. Add the shrimp and cook for as long as necessary, remembering that shrimp cook very quickly. This dish has a thick, non-runny gravy, and in India it is always served with a moong dal.

malabar shrimp curry (konju curry) *kerala*

When I visited the Taj Exotica, an immensely beautiful hotel in the Maldives, the shrimp curry was out of this world. It turned out to be the chef's mother's recipe. Her name is Baija Banu, and she is from Orumanayoor in the Malabar region of Kerala. The chef Ashfar says the secret of the flavor is the aromatic oil infusion of the mustard seed and curry leaves in the curry. Of course in Kerala, they cook fish in a terracotta pot and use coconut oil, but that has a particular taste. The shrimp in that region are ocean prawns and really fresh and large.

Serves 2

1 cup fresh grated coconut or 1 can (14fl oz) coconut milk or 1/3 cup coconut cream
1 tablespoon tamarind pulp
3 tablespoons oil
1/4 teaspoon mustard seeds
16 curry leaves
1 cup onions, sliced
1 heaped teaspoon grated ginger
3 cloves garlic
4 green chiles, cut in half lengthwise
1 whole dried red chile, broken into pieces
1 teaspoon red chile powder
1/2 teaspoon turmeric powder
1/2 teaspoon coriander powder
1/2 teaspoon cumin powder
2 chopped tomatoes
1/2 teaspoon salt
11oz uncooked peeled shrimp
2 tablespoons oil or butter
2 shallots, peeled and sliced

1 If using grated coconut, soak it in 1/2 cup of warm water in a bowl and set aside. After half an hour, squeeze out the coconut milk. Soak the tamarind in 1/2 cup of water for about an hour. Then squeeze the tamarind juice into water. Strain and set aside.

2 In a shallow pan with a handle, heat the oil and add the mustard seeds. When they start to pop, add 10 curry leaves, and after a few seconds (they let their flavor into the oil,) add the sliced onions and sauté, stirring for 5–7 minutes. Add the ginger, garlic, and green chiles. After 2 minutes, add the dried red chile and the red chile, turmeric, coriander, and cumin powders. Add 2 tablespoons of water and let the spice powders cook for a further 2 minutes, stirring so that they do not stick to the pan.

3 Add the chopped tomatoes, 1/2 cup of water, and the tamarind water. Turn the heat down and let it simmer for 5 minutes. Then add the coconut milk and salt and stir. If you want a super-smooth curry, strain it into a pan. Taste for seasoning. Add the shrimps and cook over a gentle heat until done. Shrimps cook quickly: this should only take 2–3 minutes.

4 To add a finishing touch to the curry just before serving, put 2 teaspoons of oil in a ladle and hold over the heat. When hot, add the sliced shallots, wait for 30 seconds, then add the remaining 6 curry leaves and after 10 seconds, pour the lot over the shrimp. Cover with a lid and let this aromatic infused oil seep into the curry for a few minutes. It is now ready to serve.

Best served with white rice.

shrimps with scallions and fenugreek leaves
(jheenga methi) *hyderabad*

Fish cooked in fenugreek *(methi)* leaves is a common combination in northern Indian cooking. But shrimps with fenugreek and scallions is something that I saw for the first time at the Veeraswamy restaurant in London. It had been shown to them by Mumtaz Khan of Hyderabad, who comes from a family whose table was renowned for the quality of its food.

Serves 4

1/4 cup chopped scallion
  greens (the green stem)
2 level tablespoons
  fenugreek (methi) *leaves,*
  chopped
3/4 teaspoon salt
3/4 teaspoon turmeric
  powder
3/4 teaspoon red chile
  powder
1 tablespoon lemon or lime
  juice
14oz uncooked shelled
  shrimps
3 tablespoons oil
1 cup chopped scallions
  (green and white parts)
2 green chiles, finely
  chopped
2 large cloves garlic, finely
  chopped
3/4 x 1/2-in piece of ginger,
  finely chopped
3/4 cup chopped cilantro
  leaves
1 teaspoon lime juice
  (optional)

1 Soak the scallion greens and fenugreek leaves in a bowl of water with 1/4 teaspoon of salt added. Leave to soak for 15 minutes. (This lessens the bitterness of the leaves.) Then drain, pat dry, and set aside.

2 Mix 1/4 cup of water, 1/2 teaspoon turmeric powder, the red chile powder, lemon juice, and 1/4 teaspoon of salt in a bowl. Add the shrimps, covering them well with the mixture and leave to marinate in the fridge for 30 minutes.

3 In a deep skillet, heat the oil, and when hot, add the chopped white part of the scallions, the chiles, garlic, and ginger. Sauté on a medium heat for 4–5 minutes or until the onions are translucent. Add the remaining turmeric powder and 1 tablespoon of water and cook for a further minute.

4 Add the cilantro, soaked scallion greens and fenugreek leaves and 1/4 teaspoon of salt, and stir-fry for 2 minutes.

5 Just before serving, add the shrimps, the remaining scallion greens and sauté with the soaked greens for 3 minutes or so, stirring from time to time. Add 1 cup of water, reduce the heat to low and simmer until the shrimps are cooked. Taste to check the seasoning and add a little lime juice if desired.

Serve with lemon rice and a lentil dish, as this is a dryish curry.

green fish curry (ras chawal) *parsee style*

The Parsees make various kinds of fish curry: a yellow one, a red one which has a large number of ingredients, and this green one known as *Ras Chawal* which can also be made with chicken. It is quite mild with a nice herbal taste and aroma and can be eaten with yellow rice, or just with side vegetables as in Western cuisine. If you wish, you can add a little fresh dill to the herb mixture.

Serves 2

4 teaspoons lime juice
a pinch of turmeric powder
salt
10–12oz fish fillets or steaks
1 tablespoon poppy seeds
1/2 cup coconut, grated
4–5 green chiles
1 onion, chopped
3 cloves garlic
1/4 cup cashew nuts
3 green cardamoms
1/4 blade of mace or
  1/4 teaspoon mace powder
1/4 teaspoon fennel seeds
1 1/2 cups cilantro leaves
  and stalks
a few mint leaves
1 teaspoon coriander powder
1/3 cup oil
1 teaspoon cumin seeds
1 teaspoon sugar

1 Mix half the lime juice with the turmeric, a pinch of salt, and a little water and spread over the pieces of fish. Leave to marinate for 20 minutes.

2 Pound the poppy seeds in a mortar and pestle with a little water. In a blender, grind together the coconut, chiles, onion, poppy seeds, garlic, cashew nuts, cardamoms, mace, and fennel.

3 Separately purée the cilantro leaves and mint leaves.

4 Mix the coriander powder with a little water to make a paste.

5 Heat the oil with the cumin seeds in a wide pan. When the cumin seeds begin to fry, add the coriander powder paste. After 10 seconds, add the coconut and spice paste and sauté for 7 minutes, stirring continuously, scraping off any film that forms at the bottom of the pan.

6 Add the puréed cilantro leaves and salt to taste and stir. Add the sugar and remaining lime juice. Pour in 1 1/2 cups of water and bring to a boil. Add the fish pieces and cook until done, about 7–10 minutes over a low to medium heat, depending on cut and size.

If the fish is to be eaten by itself or just with side vegetables without any rice, add 3/4 cup of water only.

You can substitute cream of coconut or coconut milk for the grated coconut. Grind the spices and cashew nuts together, and add 3/4 cup of coconut cream or milk with 3/4 cup of water after adding the fresh cilantro leaf mixture.

You can use this recipe to make a mixed vegetable curry using 9oz diced vegetables, in which case add 2 cups of water at the end and cook the vegetables until done.

crab curry *konkan coast*

This recipe is from the home of Sunita Pitamber of Mumbai, one of India's leading hostesses. The dish often graces her table. It is really hot and spicy and not for the faint-hearted. It can be made equally well with shrimps or lobster. Or even with fish, in which case the chiles need to be reduced by 20 per cent, in order not to drown the flavor of the fish.

Kashmiri chiles are good because they are mild. If using a stronger variety of chile, choose a large one with lots of skin but reduce the number depending on how hot they are. The important thing is the color and taste of the chile skin, not the "heat".

Serves 4

1 giant crab, cut into pieces, or 8 frozen crab claws
10oz coconut flesh or 1 x 14fl oz can coconut milk
1 1/2oz whole dried Kashmiri chiles, seeds and stalks removed
1/2 teaspoon turmeric powder
5 cloves garlic
1 1/2 x 1-in piece of fresh ginger
1 teaspoon poppy seeds, crushed
1 teaspoon coriander powder
1 teaspoon cumin seeds
1 onion
1oz tamarind
5 tablespoons oil
salt

1 Wash the crab well. Remove the feathery toes and the stomach sac attached to the shell just below the mouth. Take out the brown meat from the shell along with any whitish bits attached to it. Wash the main body shell to use in the curry for adding flavor. The main meat is in the claws and is white in color.

2 Cut the coconut into small pieces. Liquidize with 1 1/2 cups of water. Strain and set aside (this is the thick, first coconut milk). Once again liquidize the coconut with 2 1/2 cups of water (this is the second extract of coconut milk). Again strain and set aside. If using tinned coconut milk, dilute half with 2 cups of water and use this as second coconut milk.

3 Soak the chiles in a little warm water to soften them.

4 In a blender or food-processor, grind the chiles, turmeric powder, garlic, ginger, poppy seeds, coriander and cumin seeds, and the onion.

5 Soak the tamarind in 1 cup of warm water.

6 Heat the oil in a cooking pot and add the spice paste. Let it cook over a low heat for 15 minutes, stirring all the time. If it sticks to the pan add 1/4 cup of water. Then add the second coconut milk and simmer for 10 minutes over a very low heat. Add the crab claws and main shell with about 1 teaspoon of salt to the curry, and cook for 2 minutes. Add the tamarind water and the first coconut milk and bring to a boil immediately. Then add the brown meat with whitish attachments. Heat through and then serve.

Shrimps or fish fillets may also be used in this recipe (1lb shrimps or 1 1/2lb firm fish fillets will be ample). This is best eaten with boiled rice.

madras fish curry *coastal tamil nadu, homestyle*

Once I interviewed a cook in Bangalore, whose cooking had "magic". He came from a village near Madras and I asked him to cook for me whatever curry he would make for himself if he were at home in his village. This is what he made. It was fingerlicking good.

He said the marination of the fish in a combination of vinegar and lime juice eliminates the fishy smell, and grinding the coconut without adding water improves the taste. The gravy is pungent and quite thick.

Serves 5–6

1³/₄lb fish steaks or
  fillets, skinned
juice of ¹/₂ lime
2 teaspoons cider vinegar
salt
2 cups fresh coconut, grated
1¹/₂ x ¹/₂-in piece of
  fresh ginger
6 plump cloves garlic
1lb tomatoes,
  chopped
6 teaspoons poppy seeds,
  crushed
1¹/₂ teaspoons tamarind pulp
¹/₃ cup oil
¹/₄ teaspoon mustard seeds
2 onions, chopped
20–30 curry leaves
1 teaspoon coriander powder
¹/₂ teaspoon turmeric powder
2 teaspoons chile powder
  or paprika
³/₄ teaspoon fenugreek seeds
  and ³/₄ teaspoon cumin
  seeds, pounded together

1 Marinate the fish with the lime juice, vinegar, and a little salt for 30 minutes.

2 Put the grated coconut into a blender or food-processor with the ginger, garlic, tomatoes, and poppy seeds. Do not add any water, but process for 30 seconds.

3 Soak the tamarind in 1 cup of water for 30 minutes. Strain and set aside.

4 Heat the oil in a shallow, broad-based cooking pot and add the mustard seeds. When they pop, add the onions and fry until lightly colored, then add the curry leaves. When the onions turn golden-brown, add the coriander, turmeric, and chile powders. Stir-fry for 1 minute.

5 Add the coconut mixture and sauté for 3–4 minutes, stirring constantly. Then add the tamarind water, about ³/₄ teaspoon of salt, and a further 2 ¹/₂ cups of water. Bring to a boil and simmer for 3 minutes. Now gently lay in the fish pieces in a single layer and reduce the heat to low. Sprinkle with a mixture of the fenugreek and cumin seeds. Cook until the fish is done.

If the fish curry is made a few hours before it is required, the flavor will seep into the fish better. It is best served with boiled rice.

fish in coconut milk (fish molee) *kerala*

Fish Molee, sometimes pronounced as *Fish Moilee*, is basically an Anglo-Indian dish, a sort of fish stew. It is common among the Anglo-Indians of Mumbai, Bangalore, and Kerala, in fact all along the west coast of India. The recipes of all these communities are similar, only in Kerala local spices like cardamom, cloves, and peppercorns are used. This is truly a Raj dish.

It is a delicate-flavored curry, easy to make and always popular. It is served with white rice, though dill-flavored rice would be an interesting accompaniment. The *Molee* is nice to make with assorted *fruits de mer*.

Serves 5

1½lb small fish fillets
¼ teaspoon turmeric powder
juice of ½ lime
salt
8oz fresh coconut, grated, or
  1 x 14fl oz can coconut milk
3 tablespoons oil
1 large onion, chopped
6 green chiles, slit in half
  lengthwise
6 cloves garlic, pounded
1-in square piece of fresh
  ginger
2 small tomatoes, 1 grated
  or puréed
2 peppercorns
1 clove
2 cardamoms
6–8 curry leaves (optional)
a pinch of freshly ground
  pepper

1 Marinate the fish by mixing half of the turmeric, lime juice, and salt to taste with a little water, and then coating the fish on both sides. Leave for 15 minutes, then rinse off.

2 Soak the grated coconut in 1 cup of water, then grind in a blender. Strain and set aside the liquid. Then add 2 cups of water to the coconut in the blender and grind again. Strain the second coconut milk and reserve. (If using tinned coconut milk then dilute 1 cup with 1 cup of water to make the second extract.)

3 Heat the oil in a broad-based cooking pot and, on a low heat, sauté the onion, chiles, garlic, and ginger until the onions are lightly colored. This will take about 10 minutes. Add the tomato, peppercorns, clove, cardamoms, and curry leaves. After 2 minutes, add the second extract of coconut milk, the remaining turmeric, the puréed tomato, ground pepper, and salt to taste, and cook for 10 minutes over a low heat.

4 Add the fish pieces and the first coconut milk. Cook until the fish is done (about 3–5 minutes depending on the fish). Remove the whole spices before serving.

goa fish curry *goa*

This is Goa's signature dish, and a particular favorite in Mumbai. It is one of the best fish curries of India, and has appeal both for its taste as well as its bright orangey-red color. This color comes from the combination of Kashmiri-type chiles and a liberal use of turmeric, and also by virtue of the tamarind being ground and fried with the turmeric, which deepens its color. It is quite simple to make, but it is important to get it absolutely right by following the quantity of ingredients exactly.

The Goa curry is judged by its texture, as well as its color and taste, and the last is important. The curry should be thin and smooth in consistency and to achieve this the spices and coconut are traditionally ground several times on a grinding stone, so you would have to grind it in a food-processor for about 10 minutes for them to be satin-smooth. The favorite fish in India for use in curry is the pomfret, a flat fish. You can use halibut, cod or, surprisingly, salmon which goes well in a Goa curry. It can also be made with shrimps.

Serves 4–6

3/4lb fish, cut into pieces
  either on or off the bone
juice of 1/2 lime
3/4 teaspoon turmeric powder
salt
8 red chiles, Kashmiri-type,
  or ordinary red chiles and
  1 1/2 teaspoons paprika
4oz fresh coconut
3 teaspoons coriander seeds
2 small onions, 1 chopped,
  1 finely sliced
1 teaspoon cumin seeds
1 1/2 teaspoons chopped
  garlic
1 1/2 teaspoons tamarind pulp
2 tablespoons oil
1 tomato, grated or puréed
3 green chiles, slit
  lengthwise
a few okra (optional)
cilantro leaves, for
  garnishing

1 Marinate the fish in a mixture of the lime juice, a pinch of the turmeric powder, and a pinch of salt diluted in a little water for 30 minutes. Then rinse.

2 Soak the red chiles in 1 cup of water for 15 minutes. Strain and reserve the soaking water. In a blender or food-processor, grind the chiles (and paprika, if used), coconut, coriander seeds, the chopped onion, cumin seeds, the remaining turmeric powder, the garlic, and 1 teaspoon of tamarind pulp to make a really fine and smooth paste. Add a little of the chile soaking water to facilitate grinding, which will take 7–10 minutes for a really smooth paste. Switch off the blender once or twice so that it does not get too hot.

3 Soak the remaining 1/2 teaspoon of tamarind in 1/2 cup of water for 15 minutes. Strain and reserve the soaking water.

4 Heat the oil in a wide, shallow cooking pot and fry the finely sliced onion until it is lightly colored; this takes about 7 minutes.

5 Add the spice paste and sauté over a moderate heat for 6–7 minutes, adding a little water if necessary. The paste will become a deep orange if the chile is of good quality. When the oil begins to separate from the spices in the form of little globules on the surface of the paste, add 4 cups of water. Add the tomato, green chiles, okra, and salt to taste and cook for 6 minutes. Then taste and see if you wish to add the reserved tamarind water. Add the fish and cook until done. Sprinkle with cilantro leaves when serving.

You can keep this curry for a day in the refrigerator.

fish cooked in yogurt (doi maach) *bengal*

This is another popular fish curry from Bengal, which is usually made with carp. It is only in Bengal that you will find fish and yogurt cooked together.

Serves 4

1lb 5oz pieces of fish
1½ teaspoons salt
2 tablespoons lemon juice
½ teaspoon turmeric powder
2 teaspoons mustard powder
1½ teaspoons coriander
  powder
¾ teaspoon cumin powder
1 teaspoon red chile powder
2 teaspoons chopped ginger
2 teaspoons chopped garlic
5 tablespoons oil
½ teaspoon fenugreek seeds
1 green chile, finely chopped
2-in cinnamon stick
5 green cardamoms
3 cloves
2 medium onions, finely
  sliced
1 cup whipped plain yogurt
¾ teaspoon sugar
2 tomatoes, chopped
3 tablespoons sultanas or
  yellow seedless raisins
  (soaked in water)

1 Skin and wash the fish well. Mix ½ teaspoon of salt with the lemon juice and smear over the fish. Leave for 30 minutes, then rinse.

2 Mix all 5 spice powders and the ginger and garlic with ½ cup of water to make a spice mixture.

3 In a large saucepan, heat the oil and add the fenugreek seeds, chopped green chile, cinnamon, and cardamoms. After 30 seconds, add the cloves. After 10 seconds, add the onions and fry till light brown (this will take about 10 minutes). Add the spice mixture and cook on a low heat until most of the moisture has dried up. Then sauté the spices for 2 more minutes, stirring continuously.

4 Add 2 tablespoons water and cook for 1 minute, then pour in 2 cups of water and simmer for 10 minutes, so that the onions soften and the spices cook properly.

5 Turn the heat down very low, add the whipped yogurt, and stir continuously for 5 minutes. Add the sugar, tomatoes, and up to 1 cup of water, depending on the gravy required, and 1 teaspoon of salt and stir well. Put the fish in gently and cook for 3 minutes, uncovered, before turning the pieces over. Add the sultanas after 3 minutes and cook, uncovered, until the fish is perfectly done.

mango and yogurt curry *gujarat*

In the mango season, which is in the summer in India, the Gujaratis eat the fruit as part of their main meal. They eat mango juice with puris. Then, in order not to waste the pulp around the skin and the seed, they use this to flavor a yogurt curry and in fact boil the mango seed in it. This curry is known colloquially as *fajeta,* an odd name because it means something to be made fun of, or a joke! The seed and the inside of the mango skin is washed very thoroughly to remove every trace of the mango pulp, so as to avoid even a tiny bit of wastage, and this is the *raison d'être* of the curry.

This is a tasty curry, and the recipe is straightforward. The proper quantity of mango must be used to get the best results. The variety of mango normally used for this dish in India is the sweet, inexpensive *pairi*, but it can be made with any sweet mango, or even frozen pulp.

The curry should be eaten with boiled rice or parathas. It can also be served as a side dish instead of a lentil dal. Mango curry is traditionally eaten only at lunch-time because mango is considered heavy to digest–the ginger and asafoetida aid digestion. This curry also makes a wonderful soup.

Serves 4

3 cups sweet (fully ripe)
  mangoes or mango pulp,
  to make mango juice
4^1/$_2$ tablespoons plain yogurt
3 tablespoons gram flour
  (besan)
^{3}/$_4$ teaspoon ginger powder
a pinch of asafoetida
  (optional)
1–2 green chiles
2 teaspoons ginger purée
1 tablespoon oil
1 teaspoon cumin seeds
8 curry leaves
salt
jaggery or cane sugar
  (optional)

1 Soak the mangoes in water for 15 minutes. Roll each mango between both hands, pressing them in the process in order to soften them. When they feel softened, press the area around the stalk end, then make a small hole at the top of the fruit by removing the stalk end. In a large strainer set over a bowl, squeeze out the juice by pressing or rolling the mango between both hands. When all the juice is out, press the pulp in the strainer with a spoon to extract any remaining juice. The mango juice for this curry must be smooth, without any fibre.

2 Whisk the yogurt until smooth. Whisking prevents the yogurt from curdling while cooking.

3 Put the gram flour into a small bowl, add 1 cup of water, and mix to a very smooth paste without any lumps.

4 Put the mango juice, yogurt, and gram flour paste into a cooking pot and mix well, using a whisk if necessary. Strain. Add a further 2 cups of water, and the ginger powder and asafoetida.

5 In a herb mill, purée the chiles with the ginger purée and add to the mango and yogurt mixture with about 2 teaspoons of salt. Cook over a low heat for 15 minutes, stirring from time to time.

6 Heat the oil in a very small skillet or stainless steel ladle that can be held over a very low heat. When hot, add the cumin seeds and fry for just 10 seconds, then add the curry leaves and fry for 6–7 seconds, and add along with the hot oil to the curry mixture. Let this cook for a further 15 minutes, stirring from time to time.

7 Taste for salt and sweetness and add more salt if necessary, and sugar if desired. If using jaggery, break off a small piece, equivalent to a teaspoonful and add; it will soon melt into the curry.

watermelon curry (matira curry) *rajasthan*

This recipe is from Rajasthan. In the summer, temperatures in this arid desert region exceed 100°F and in the old days, before foodstuffs from other regions were easily available, the Rajasthani had to rely on what was locally available. Watermelons, called *matira* in Rajasthan, were one of the few fruits available in the summer, and are used to make an interesting semi-dry curry.

The flavor should be hot, sweet, and sour, hence the large amount of chile powder—and Rajasthan chile is pungent. You can substitute paprika, which is milder. This is quite interesting to eat with rice, or as a side dish.

Serves 2
Serves 4 as a side dish

$^1/_4$ *large watermelon*
1$^1/_2$ teaspoons red chile
powder
a pinch of turmeric powder
$^1/_2$ teaspoon coriander
powder
1 teaspoon garlic purée
salt
2 tablespoons oil
$^1/_4$ teaspoon cumin seeds
sugar to taste (optional)
2–3 teaspoons lime juice

1 Cut up the watermelon and remove the seeds. Peel off the skin and chop the flesh into 1$^1/_2$-in cubes. Take 1 cup of the chopped watermelon and blend it to make juice. To the juice add the chile, turmeric and coriander powders, garlic purée, and salt to taste.

2 Heat the oil in a wok, add the cumin seeds and within 20 seconds, add the watermelon juice mixture. Lower the heat and simmer for 5 minutes or so, so that the spices cook completely and the liquid is reduced by a third. If using sugar, add it now, then add the lime juice and cook for 1 minute.

3 Add the remaining chopped watermelon and cook over a low heat for 3–4 minutes, gently tossing it until all the pieces are covered in the spice mixture.

mixed dried fruit curry (dry fruit korma) *mumbai*

The Taj Mahal Hotel in Mumbai has a magnificent ballroom where for several decades a lavish lunch used to be served every day, against the backdrop of a live orchestra. As life moved on from the age of leisure to one of practicality, the daily buffet lunch died a natural death in the late 1980s.

The buffet used to have a separate section for vegetarian food, both Indian and Western. Occasionally a version of this curry used to feature in it. It is one of my favorites.

I have adapted the recipe to make it more full-bodied, although it is still mild. This is an ideal dish to serve on an important occasion when you want to prepare a vegetarian curry meal, or as a side dish, in which case reduce the amount of water added towards the end. As a main course, serve with yellow or saffron rice.

Serves 4–5

4oz dried Hunza apricots
3/4 cup almonds, blanched
1/2 cup pistachios
3/4 cup cashew nuts
1 1/2 cups plain yogurt
salt
1/2 teaspoon ground white
  pepper
4 tablespoons oil
1 cinnamon or bay leaf
2-in cinnamon stick
3 cloves
4 green cardamoms
3 medium onions, finely
  chopped
1 x 1/2-in piece of fresh
  ginger, chopped
4 cloves garlic, chopped
4 green chiles, chopped
1 teaspoon coriander powder
1/2 teaspoon cumin powder
1 teaspoon red chile powder
  or paprika
2 tomatoes, chopped
3 tablespoons ghee
1/2 cup walnut pieces
3/4 cup seedless yellow raisins
1/4 teaspoon garam masala
  powder
3 tablespoons light cream
a few maraschino cherries,
  to garnish

1 Soak the apricots in water for 1 1/2 hours, then slit and remove the stones (if unpitted).

2 Soak the almonds and pistachios in hot water for 1 hour. Remove the skins. Reserve the soaking water for use in the curry.

3 Grind half the cashew nuts with a little water to make a paste.

4 Whisk the yogurt, adding 1/4 teaspoon of salt and the white pepper.

5 Heat the oil in a skillet with the cinnamon or bay leaf, cinnamon, cloves, and cardamoms. Add the onions and fry until medium-brown. This will take about 20 minutes. Add the ginger, garlic, and chiles and sauté for 5 minutes. By now the onions should be dark brown. It is important for the taste and appearance of the dish that the onions should fry to a deep brown—almost *café au lait* in color.

6 Add the coriander powder and sauté for 3–4 minutes, then add the cumin and red chile powders, stirring continuously. After a minute add the tomatoes and sauté for 2–3 minutes.

7 Remove from the heat and cool. Remove the cinnamon leaf, put the mixture into a blender, and purée. Then pour into a cooking pot. Add the whisked yogurt, cashew paste, and 2 cups of water, with salt to taste. Cover, and simmer for 15 minutes.

8 Meanwhile, heat the ghee in a skillet and fry the almonds, remaining cashew nuts, walnut pieces, raisins, apricots, and most of the pistachios for 6–7 minutes, reserving a few for the garnish.

9 Add the nuts and fruit mixture to the gravy and cook, covered, on a low heat for 15 minutes. Sprinkle with garam masala powder and cook for a further 5 minutes until the nuts are tender.

10 Garnish with swirls of cream, flaked pistachios, and maraschino cherries just before serving.

egg curry (egg kurma) *chettinad*

In every part of India a curry with hard-boiled eggs is made by using the most common homestyle curry recipe of the region and adding hard-boiled eggs when it is ready. It is served when unexpected guests arrive as well as providing an acceptable protein curry for children.

In some parts of India, however, particularly in the Malabar and Chettinad regions, an egg curry is actually considered an important part of the cuisine. This recipe (adapted) is from the home of Mr M. A. Ramaswamy, who is the Raja of Chettinad, as shown to me by his wife, Sigapi Ramaswamy.

Serves 4

6 eggs, hard-boiled
3 teaspoons coriander
  powder
1¹/2 teaspoons chile powder
  or paprika
1 teaspoon fennel seeds
1 teaspoon cumin seeds
¹/2 teaspoon turmeric powder
¹/2 x ¹/4-in piece of fresh
  ginger
2 plump cloves garlic
¹/2 fresh coconut, grated, or
  1 cup desiccated coconut, or
  1 x 7fl oz can of
  coconut milk
2 tablespoons oil
¹/2 teaspoon fenugreek seeds
¹/2 teaspoon fennel seeds
2-in cinnamon stick
8oz onions, finely chopped
8oz tomatoes, finely chopped
salt
juice of ¹/2 lime

1 Peel the eggs and halve them lengthwise.

2 Put the coriander powder, chile powder or paprika, fennel and cumin seeds, turmeric powder, ginger, and garlic into a blender with 2 tablespoons of water and purée to a thick paste.

3 Put the coconut into a blender with 2 cups of warm water. Liquidize, then strain the coconut milk and set aside.

4 Heat the oil in a cooking pot and fry the fenugreek seeds, fennel seeds, and the cinnamon for 10 seconds. Add the onion and fry until lightly colored. Add the spice paste and sauté for 7 minutes. (It will darken in color since it contains a lot of coriander.) Add a few drops of water if it sticks to the bottom of the pot. Then add the tomatoes and sauté for 2–3 minutes.

5 Add 3 cups of warm water with salt to taste, cover, and simmer for 20 minutes, to make a smooth gravy. Just before serving, add 2 cups of the coconut milk and bring to a boil. Add the lime juice, taste and add more salt if necessary, and gently lay in the hard-boiled eggs with the yellow facing upwards. Carefully scoop into a serving dish.

If you want to freeze this curry, omit the coconut and eggs, but add lime juice and salt, and freeze. Then use it to make egg curry as and when you need, topping it with coconut milk at the time of reheating.

omelette curry *malabar coast*

The Muslims and the Parsees are very fond of eggs. The Parsees have many ways of preparing them, and the Muslims of each part of India have very interesting egg dishes which are not found elsewhere. The Muslims of the Malabar Coast in northern Kerala make a curry made with an omelette cut into broad strips. The gravy is like a thick spicy coating around the omelette strips.

This is best eaten with sliced bread as an ideal dish for brunch or high tea. This recipe is from Umni Abdulla, who is an expert in the cuisine of this region.

Serves 3

For the omelette
3 free-range eggs
1 small onion, finely chopped
2 green chiles, finely chopped
1 teaspoon chopped
   cilantro leaves
a pinch of ground pepper
salt
oil

For the curry
2 tablespoons grated coconut
$^1/_2$ teaspoon cumin seeds
$^1/_2$ teaspoon fennel seeds
2 teaspoons coriander
   powder
$^1/_2$ teaspoon red chile powder
$^1/_4$ teaspoon turmeric powder
$^1/_2$ teaspoon garam masala
   powder
2 tablespoons oil
3 small onions, finely sliced
2–3 green chiles, chopped
2 medium tomatoes, chopped
1 teaspoon cider vinegar
1 tablespoon chopped
   cilantro leaves
salt

1 Put the coconut, cumin and fennel seeds, coriander, red chile, turmeric, and garam masala powders into a blender with 2 tablespoons of water and grind to a paste. Set aside.

2 To make the omelette, whisk the eggs. Add the onion, green chiles, cilantro leaves, pepper, and salt to taste and mix well.

3 Heat a little oil in a large pan and, when hot, pour in the egg and chile mixture.

4 When the lower side of the omelette is cooked, turn the omelette over with a large spatula. Let the other side cook, then remove from the heat. First cut the omelette in half, then cut crosswise into 1-in wide strips. Roll up the strips. Set aside on kitchen paper.

5 To make the curry, heat the oil in the skillet and fry the sliced onions over a moderate heat for 10 minutes. Add the spice paste and fry for 3–4 minutes. Add a little more oil if the mixture sticks to the pan but the spices must fry properly.

6 Add the green chiles and tomatoes and sauté for 5 minutes. Then add the vinegar, 3 cups of water, and salt to taste. Simmer for 10 minutes.

7 Add the cilantro leaves and omelette strips. Cook for 3 minutes over a very low heat, then serve.

eggplant curry *kerala*

This is a homestyle curry from Kerala. The traditional way of cooking anything with tamarind is in a terracotta dish, and the terracotta in Kerala is often of the black variety.

This curry is hot with a sour tang to it. Very tasty, it is best with a flavored rice like lemon rice or dill rice, and fried south Indian papadams.

Serves 4

1 1/2 oz tamarind pulp
1 lb baby eggplants
salt
1/2 fresh coconut, grated, or
  5 oz frozen
6 whole red chiles
1 teaspoon coriander seeds
1/2 teaspoon cumin seeds
4 tablespoons oil
1/4 teaspoon mustard seeds
1 teaspoon chopped garlic
1 teaspoon fresh ginger,
  chopped
8–10 curry leaves
2 onions, chopped
1/4 teaspoon turmeric powder
1 tablespoon chopped
  cilantro leaves

1 Soak the tamarind in 1/2 cup of hot water for at least 30 minutes.

2 Make 2 incisions, like a cross, halfway up each eggplant. Cut off the stems. Soak the eggplants in water with a pinch of salt for 15 minutes, to reduce the natural bitterness.

3 On a heated griddle, toast the coconut for 5–6 minutes, then add the chiles and coriander seeds and toast for 2–3 minutes. Add the cumin and toast for 1 minute. Put into a small grinder and grind to a paste, adding a little water.

4 Heat the oil in a cooking pot and add the mustard seeds. When they pop, add the garlic, ginger, and curry leaves, then the onions and turmeric. After 25 minutes add the spice paste and sauté for a further 10–15 minutes, adding a little water if the spices stick.

5 Add 2 cups of water, and stir well add salt to taste (about 1 1/4 teaspoons), and the eggplants, then cover. After 15 minutes add the tamarind water (after squeezing the tamarind and straining it). Cook until the eggplants are tender, then remove from the heat and sprinkle with cilantro leaves when serving.

cauliflower and potato curry
(cauliflower gashi) *mangalore*

In north India the cauliflower is usually cooked as a dry vegetable, rarely as a curry. However on the west coast of India, around Mangalore, the Hindu community do make a curry with it (called a *gashi*), combining it with large pieces of potato. It is actually very tasty. Serve with white rice.

Serves 3

1½ cups chopped fresh
  coconut
7–8 tablespoons oil
1½ onions, chopped
5 dried red chiles
2 teaspoons coriander seeds
⅛ teaspoon mustard seeds
⅛ teaspoon fenugreek seeds
¼ teaspoon cumin seeds
1-in cinnamon stick
4 peppercorns
2 cloves
½ teaspoon turmeric
½ teaspoon paprika powder
1 heaped teaspoon tamarind
¾ x ½-in piece of fresh
  ginger, finely chopped
4 cloves garlic, finely chopped
7oz potatoes, peeled and
  chopped into large pieces
salt
14oz cauliflower, cut into
  large florets

1 Soak 1 cup of coconut in 2 cups of warm water. Leave for 30 minutes, then put into a blender. Strain and reserve the coconut milk.

2 In a non-stick skillet, heat 1 tablespoon of oil and sauté the remaining chopped coconut for 2–3 minutes. Set aside.

3 Heat another tablespoon of oil and sauté half the onions for 2–3 minutes. Set aside.

4 Heat 1 more tablespoon of oil and sauté the red chiles, coriander, mustard, fenugreek and cumin seeds, cinnamon, peppercorns, and cloves for 30 seconds, and remove.

5 Now put the coconut, onions, and spices into a blender. Add the turmeric, paprika and tamarind and ½ cup of water and grind to a smooth paste.

6 In a saucepan, heat 4 tablespoons of oil and sauté the ginger and garlic for 15 seconds, followed by the balance of the chopped onions for about 7–8 minutes, until translucent. Add the spice paste, sauté for 2 minutes, then add a little water and the potatoes and sauté for about 5 minutes. Sprinkle in the salt (about 1 teaspoon). Add ½ cup of water, cover, and cook for 6–7 minutes.

7 Now add the cauliflower and 2 cups of coconut milk and cook until done.

As I suggest in the section on menus, if some of your guests are vegetarian, you can make extra of the spice paste for Chicken in Thick Coconut Gravy (see page 116) and cook this cauliflower curry for the non-meat eaters. The spice mix is very similar to the one above, but normally slightly less spices are used when making a vegetable dish like this one.

mixed vegetable curry (kath katha) *goa*

There are hundreds of ways of making mixed vegetable curry. Almost every recipe in this book can be adapted to cook vegetables instead of lamb, chicken, or fish.

This is a Hindu Goan curry. While the Goa Fish Curry (see page 140) is eaten by the Hindu and Christians of Goa alike, the Hindus alone make a vegetable curry.

Serves 4

2 onions
4 tablespoons oil
1 cup grated coconut
6 dried red chiles
2 tablespoons coriander
 seeds
4 cloves
10 peppercorns
2-in cinnamon stick
¹/₂ teaspoon mustard seeds
¹/₃ teaspoon cumin seeds
¹/₄ teaspoon asafoetida
 (optional)
¹/₄ teaspoon turmeric powder
1 cinnamon or bay leaf
1 blade of mace
salt
1lb diced mixed vegetables
 (yam, carrots, potato, sweet
 potato, beans, peas)
1 teaspoon lime or lemon
 juice

1 Chop 1 onion finely and slice the other.

2 Put 1 tablespoon of oil into a non-stick skillet, add the grated coconut, and sauté for 5 minutes. Remove and set aside in a bowl.

3 Put the red chiles and coriander seeds into the same pan. After 3 minutes, add the cloves, peppercorns, and cinnamon and stir for 2–3 minutes. Remove and add to the coconut in the bowl.

4 In a blender, purée the coconut, roasted spices, and sliced onion, adding ¹/₂ cup of water.

5 Heat the remaining oil in a cooking pot, and add the mustard seeds, cumin seeds, asafoetida, and turmeric powder. After a minute, add the cinnamon or bay leaf and chopped onion and fry for 20–25 minutes, or until the onion is browned. Add the spice mix and the mace and fry for 10–12 minutes. Pour in 3 cups of water, add salt to taste, and mix well.

6 Now add the vegetables in order of their cooking time. Start with the yam, followed after 10 minutes by carrots and 5 minutes later by the potato and sweet potato, followed after 5 minutes by the beans. Finally add the peas.

7 Cook, uncovered, over a low heat until the vegetables are tender. Then add the lime or lemon juice.

pineapple curry (annas curry) *mangalore*

In India pineapples grow in Assam and along the west coast. In the latter region—Kerala, Goa, and Mangalore— many fruits, for example, bananas, mangoes, jackfruit, and pineapple are made into savory dishes. This recipe is from the Brahmin community of Mangalore.

Serves 4

1 cup grated coconut
1lb fresh pineapple,
   peeled and cubed
1/4 teaspoon mustard powder
2 green chiles
1/2 teaspoon salt
2 tablespoons oil, butter or
   ghee
a pinch of mustard seeds
12 curry leaves
2 red chiles. broken into
   pieces
1 tablespoon chopped
   cilantro leaves

For the marinade

1/3 teaspoon mustard powder
1/4 teaspoon turmeric powder
11/2–2 teaspoons sugar
   (depending on the sourness
   of the pineapple)
1/4 teaspoon salt

1 Put half of the grated coconut in a bowl with 2/3 cup of warm water and set aside for 15 minutes. Then squeeze out the coconut milk—you should get about 1/2 cup.

2 Put the pineapple into a bowl. Mix the marinade ingredients and a little water in a small bowl and sprinkle over all the pineapple. Mix well. Leave to marinate for at least 15 minutes.

3 Put the remaining grated coconut, mustard powder, green chiles (without stem), salt, and 1 cup of water into a blender and purée.

4 Heat the oil in a shallow pan. When smoking hot, add the mustard seeds and when they pop, add the curry leaves and stir. They will release their fragrance into the oil. After a minute or so, add the red chiles and stir. After a few seconds (and before the red chiles turn very dark,) add the pineapple. Stir-fry for 10 minutes.

5 Add the puréed coconut mixture and the coconut milk. Taste for seasoning and adjust the salt and sugar if necessary. Cook for 5 minutes, or until preferred texture of pineapple is reached. Garnish with cilantro leaves to serve.

Best with white rice and accompanied by a vegetable such as potatoes with spinach or fenugreek.

creamy potato curry (malaidhar aloo) *lucknow*

In the last twenty years India has had what we call a "white revolution"—the growth of the dairy industry. India is now the world's second largest producer of milk! Side by side with the rise in consumption of milk products, Indians have taken a liking to cooking Indian food with cheese. Traditionally, of course, they have always loved cooking with ghee and butter. This is a newly created dish by a master chef from Lucknow, Imtiaz Quereshi, though I have altered it slightly.

Serves 5 as a side dish

1 1/4lb medium potatoes
  (about 3-in long)
1/4 teaspoon turmeric
1 teaspoon salt
juice of 1/4 lime or 1/4 lemon
2 cups plain yogurt
1/4 pint light cream
1 1/2 tablespoons finely
  chopped fresh ginger
4 cloves garlic
1 tablespoon finely chopped
  green chiles
1 teaspoon salt
1/4 teaspoon mace powder
1/4 teaspoon cardamom
  powder
1 teaspoon sugar
2 teaspoons butter
1 teaspoon ground
  black pepper
3 tablespoon grated Cheddar
  cheese
1/2 cup finely chopped onion
1/2 teaspoon black cumin
  seeds (shahjeera)—optional
1 tablespoon chopped mint
  leaves

1 Peel the potatoes and cut into slices across the width, about 2/3-in thick. Parboil in a pan of boiling water with the turmeric, salt, and lime juice. Remove from the heat after 3 minutes and drain. Fill with cold tap water to cool the potatoes, then drain the water again. Prick the potatoes gently with a fork.

2 Make the marinade in a separate cooking pot: put in the yogurt, then beat or whisk it. Add the cream, ginger, garlic, green chiles, and salt. Add the potatoes and leave for at least 15 minutes.

3 Put this pot over a low heat and add the mace powder, cardamom powder, sugar, butter, pepper, cheese, and chopped onion. Stir, then add 1 1/2 cups of water. Bring to a simmer and add the black cumin seeds.

4 Cook, uncovered, on a very low heat until the potatoes are done (about 5–7 minutes). When serving, you can reheat in the same pot, or put into an oven-proof casserole dish and reheat just before serving. To finish, sprinkle the chopped fresh mint over the top.

Best as part of an Indian meal with rice or roti, along with another dryish meat, fish, or vegetarian dish. Can also be baked instead of cooked, and served as part of a Western meal.

chickpea curry (chanas or chole) *sindhi style*

Chickpeas are known as *kabuli chanas* or grams from Kabul. They are popular among Punjabis who call them *chole,* and eat them with flour pancakes, *bathuras.* They are made in a sort of blackish spice mix with a dominant flavor of cumin. The Sindhis eat this curry too, but heaped on sliced bread, and the flavor has a slightly sour tang. It can be eaten as a centrepiece with roti, rice, or bread, or as a side dish instead of dal. If you are using raw chickpeas, you must soak them the night before. Tinned chickpeas can be used instead; you will need 2 x 1lb cans.

Serves 6 as a main course
Serves 8 as a side dish

1/3 cup dried chickpeas
3 large onions
1/2oz fresh ginger
1/2oz garlic
2 small tomatoes, skinned
  and de-seeded
2 black cardamoms
8 cloves
2 cinnamon or bay leaves
15 peppercorns
1 teaspoon cumin seeds
salt
a pinch of asafoetida
1/3 cup oil
1 teaspoon turmeric powder
1/2 teaspoon garam masala
  powder
1 teaspoon coriander powder
1/2 teaspoon ground black
  pepper
3/4 teaspoon dried mango
  powder (amchoor)

1 Soak the chickpeas overnight in 5 cups of water (if you will be cooking in a pressure cooker, use 4 cups).

2 Chop 2 of the onions and reserve. In a food-processor, purée another onion with the ginger and garlic. Purée the tomatoes separately.

3 Place the soaked chickpeas (and the soaking water) in a pressure cooker or ordinary cooking pot, with the last chopped onion, the black cardamoms, cloves, cinnamon or bay leaves, peppercorns, cumin seeds, 1 teaspoon of salt, and the asafoetida. Bring to a boil. Cook for 20 minutes in a pressure cooker or if using an ordinary pot, for at least 50 minutes. Drain and reserve the cooking liquid.

4 In a separate cooking pot, heat the oil. Add the reserved chopped onion and sauté for 25 minutes, or until brown. Add the puréed onion, ginger, and garlic mixture and sauté for 10 minutes. (If using tinned chickpeas, add now and fry with the puréed onion.)

5 Add the turmeric, garam masala, and coriander powders, pepper, and mango powder and stir thoroughly. After 1 minute, add the puréed tomato and sauté for a few minutes.

6 Add the cooked chickpeas and stir gently. Add the water in which the chickpeas were cooked (you can strain away the spices since their flavor is already extracted) and cook until tender. Add salt to taste at the end of cooking.

sindhi curry (sindhi besan ka curry) *mumbai*

This is a curry made from just a few teaspoons of gram flour (you can substitute with §wholewheat flour oratta). It is a famous dish of the Sindhi community and is usually eaten for Sunday lunch with boiled rice and fried potatoes called *took*. This curry is full of vegetables and lentils, thus an ideal dish to make for vegetarian guests, and the consistency is that of a thin dal. It is also quite nice just as a soup—simply add a spoonful of boiled rice when serving. This curry is considered heavy to digest, so is always eaten at lunchtime.

Serves 6

1 1/2 teaspoons tamarind
 pulp
6 cocum pieces (optional)
2–3 medium potatoes
1 small carrot
10–12 okra
6 green chiles
4 baby eggplants
5oz yam
1/3 cup oil
1 teaspoon fenugreek seeds
1 teaspoon cumin seeds
2 teaspoons fresh ginger,
 finely chopped
about 12 curry leaves
1/4 teaspoon asafoetida
1/3 cup gram flour (or
 wholewheat flour)
1 teaspoon red chile powder
1 teaspoon turmeric powder
12–15 cluster beans (gowar)
 or thin French beans
salt
1 heaped teaspoon sugar
8 mint leaves
1 tablespoon cilantro
 leaves, chopped

1 Soak the tamarind in 1/2 cup of water and, separately, the cocum, in 1/2 cup of water, each for 30 minutes.

2 Scrub the potatoes. Cut into quarters or chunks if using large potatoes. You can leave the skin on. Scrape the carrot and cut into 1 1/2-in thick strips. Trim the stem from the okra but leave a stub or the okra will become mushy when cooking. Chop 2 of the green chiles. Cut the eggplants in half lengthwise. Peel and cube the yam.

3 Using a cooking pot of at least 5 pint capacity, heat 4 tablespoons of oil and add the fenugreek seeds followed by the cumin seeds. After 30 seconds, add the ginger, chopped green chiles, and curry leaves.

4 Fry for a minute, then add the asafoetida and gram or wholewheat flour. Stir continuously for 4–5 minutes. The flour will absorb the oil and form a paste, but you must stir it now in order to give body to the taste. Turn the heat down low and sauté properly.

5 Add the chile and turmeric powders and another tablespoon of oil and sauté for 2–3 minutes. Then add 8 cups of hot water, stirring continuously until the paste dissolves in the water. Bring to a boil and simmer for 10 minutes.

6 Add the vegetables (the yam first, followed 10 minutes later by the potatoes and 5 minutes later by the other vegetables), with salt, sugar, the 4 whole green chiles, tamarind water, cocum, and cocum water. Boil until the vegetables are cooked. Then add the mint and cilantro leaves. The curry will thicken slightly on cooking.

The whole green chiles are for those who like to eat chiles whole. If serving as a soup, leave out the whole chiles. This curry should be eaten with rice.

rice

Rice is the staple food of roughly half of India. It is grown typically in the delta areas and beside rivers, in irrigated areas and where the monsoons bring heavy rains. Rice supposedly originated in upper Thailand and north-east India. Fields are flooded with a few inches of water when the rice seedlings are transplanted and need to be well-watered until just before harvest. In some areas of India, only one crop per year is raised, while in areas where water is not a problem nowadays two crops per year are common. About 45 million hectares yield 80 million tonnes of rice per year. There is no part of India that does not have rice as an important feature of its cuisine. Boiled rice is eaten with curries, dals, yogurt, and vegetables throughout India. It is made into flour and rotis (griddle-made breads) are made from rice in Kerala. It is ground to make staple snack foods such as *dosas* and *idlis* all over the south. It is used to make desserts such as *mutaranjan,* which are the sweet pulaos of the Muslims, and *kheer*, a Hindu rice pudding.

Each part of India grows its own variety of rice, which is largely consumed in the region. The most popular kinds of rice, apart from Basmati, are the *jeera* (short, fine-grain, like the cumin seed after which it is named; *jeera* meaning cumin), *golden sela* (which is grown in Northern India and is a thicker long grain rice with a golden hue, very good for making pulaos as the grains retain their identity), *ambe mohue,* which has a hint of mango fragrance (*ambe* meaning mango) and is grown in Maharashtra, and *punni,* a long grain rice, which comes from Tamil Nadu. On the coast of southern India, parboiled rice is the staple food.

Basmati is the king of rice. It is famous not only for its very long, slim grain, which lengthens even further during cooking, but for its aroma. It is said that the species was originally brought from Afghanistan and planted in the hills of Dehra Dun, to the north-west of Delhi, where it benefits from the cool air at harvesting time. Now, of course, Basmati rice is grown all over the Punjab, the neighbouring state of Haryana, and in the foothills of the Himalayas, in an area known as Terai, in Uttar Pradesh. India exports Basmati rice to the UK, the US and the Middle East. It loses its aroma with too much polishing in an effort to make it extra white in color. In the days of the Raj it was called Patna rice. Basmati rice is now cultivated in Pakistan, Thailand and the US. When buying it, be aware that all long grain rice is not Basmati rice.

Basmati can be used for biryanis and on special occasions as it is much more expensive than ordinary rice. To make perfect rice, the grains should be at least a year old. Many households store rice for a year, mixing a little oil into it to discourage insects. It is possible to buy older rice in markets, though the price is a bit higher. It is a pity that year-old Basmati rice is not marketed in the West.

cooking rice

There are two ways to do this: one is the pasta way—you boil a lot of water, a pinch of salt, and a few drops of oil, add the rice and when tender pour out the excess water. In rural India this is how rice is prepared—in bulbous-shaped pots with a narrow neck, to facilitate pouring off the excess water, to keep the heat in afterwards, and to slowly dry out the excess moisture.

The second way of cooking rice is the absorption method, in which you put exactly the amount of water required to be absorbed to give the rice a perfect consistency. It is difficult to be accurate because the exact amount of water depends on the variety of rice used, its age, and so on.

Always use a pot that will be three-quarters full when the rice is cooked—and rice expands substantially. If the rice just about fits the pot, it will be inhibited from fully fluffing up. Allow 1/2 cup of raw rice per person. If cooking for a party of 6–8, add an additional 1/2 cup in case some of your guests are indulgent.

In the Far East, electric rice cookers are used and they keep the rice warm without it going soggy. It is an effective way of cooking rice, but you need to put in the correct amount of water.

Rice is supposed to cool the body and, in the summer, it is eaten for both lunch and dinner. In the winter, in colder Northern India, rice would not normally be served at night but, in the warmer south, it is eaten throughout the year. Rice is easy to digest and is given to convalescent people.

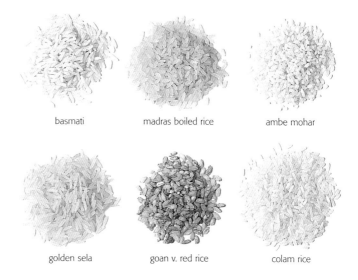

basmati   madras boiled rice   ambe mohar

golden sela   goan v. red rice   colam rice

boiled rice for 2

1 cup rice
1 1/3 cups water, if using Basmati (or follow packet instructions)
salt
a few drops of oil

It is best to cook the rice about 1 hour before the start of a meal. Wash the rice twice, throw away the water, then soak the rice for about 15–20 minutes. The rice will expand 25 per cent in this time. The exact quantity of water to be used depends on the variety of rice. For Basmati, a rough guide is 1 1/3 times the quantity of rice. Put the water on to boil in a large pot, add salt (about 1/6 teaspoon per cup of rice) and a few drops of oil, and when boiling add the rice and cook until 95 per cent done (around 10 minutes' boiling time for Basmati). Add a little extra hot water if necessary, then reduce the heat as low as possible, and remove the pot from the heat. Put a griddle, crêpe pan, or skillet over the heat and put the rice pan on top. Cover. This will create a gentle heat and prevents the rice sticking to the bottom of the pot. Let the rice finish cooking in its own steam. When perfectly done, turn off the heat and remove the lid to allow excess moisture to evaporate. Stir gently with a fork to enable the rice to dry and give you perfectly cooked rice with separated grains.

You can season the rice with cumin seeds that have been fried in 2 tablespoons of butter, ghee, or oil in a ladle for 30 seconds. Sprinkle over the rice when in its serving dish.

fragrant rice
When boiling rice, add 1/2-in cinnamon stick and 1/4 bay leaf, together with 1 cardamom and 1 clove, if liked. Remove the spices before serving.

yellow rice
This rice can be served whenever you choose as the taste and flavor do not alter, only the color. Just add a pinch of turmeric when boiling the rice.

saffron rice
Soak a few strands of saffron in 3 tablespoons of water for 30 minutes. When the rice is done, pour the soaking water and the saffron over the cooked rice with a teaspoon and return the lid to the pot so that the aroma does not escape.

yellow and white rice (biryani rice)

When you eat biryani in restaurants you may have noticed the two-colored, deep yellow and white rice. Well, there is a simple trick to this. Restaurateurs pour a few drops of yellow liquid food coloring randomly over the rice in the cooking pot when it is finally done. This color then seeps down, resulting in a mixture of yellow and white rice when served. You can also add a few drops of green coloring and get three-colored rice.

pulao rice

For 1 cup of pulao rice, slice 1 small onion finely. Then heat 2 tablespoons of oil in the pot in which you will cook the rice, and fry the onions until deep brown. Add the rice, a small piece of bay leaf, ¹/₂-in cinnamon stick, and 1 clove and sauté for 2 minutes. Then cook the rice as explained on page 171.

lemon rice

1 cup rice
8 cashew nuts
¹/₈ teaspoon turmeric powder
salt
3 tablespoons oil
1 green chile, finely chopped
¹/₄ teaspoon mustard seeds
10 curry leaves
juice of ¹/₂ lemon or 1 lime

1 Wash the rice 2 or 3 times in fresh water. Then soak for 30 minutes.

2 Meanwhile, soak the cashew nuts in 1 cup of water for 15 minutes.

3 Bring water equal to 1¹/₄ times the volume of rice to a boil in a pot. When boiling, add the rice, turmeric powder, and ¹/₄ teaspoon of salt. The rice should be cooked in 11 minutes, when all the liquid should be absorbed. Turn off the heat, remove the rice, and spread in a flat dish or pan to cool and dry. Leave for 30 minutes.

4 In a wok or large skillet, heat the oil. Fry the chile for 1 minute, then add the mustard seeds, drained cashew nuts, and curry leaves and fry for 30 seconds. Add the lemon or lime juice. Add the cooked rice and stir well but carefully with a flat spatula so as not to mash the rice. The rice is now ready to serve.

fried browned rice

3 cups rice
5 tablespoons oil
2 medium onions, thinly sliced
1/2-in cinnamon stick
1 bay leaf
6 cloves
1/2 blade of mace (optional)
2 teaspoons sugar
salt

1 Soak the rice for 15 minutes. Wash well and drain.

2 Heat the oil in a pot and fry the onions until brown. Add the cinnamon, bay leaf, cloves, and mace and sauté for 5 minutes. Add the sugar and let it caramelize. Add the rice and sauté for 2 minutes. Add salt to taste (about 1 teaspoon) and 4 cups of boiling water, and cook for 9–10 minutes until the rice is perfectly cooked.

dill rice (sooaa chawal)

1 cup rice
3 tablespoons oil
2 green cardamoms
1/2–1 green chile, finely chopped (optional)
1/3 cup finely chopped fresh dill
salt

1 Wash and soak the rice.

2 Heat the oil in a cooking pot and fry the cardamoms and green chile for 1 minute. Then add the dill and a little salt and sauté over a low heat for 2 minutes. Add the rice and sauté for 1 minute. Then add 1 1/4 cups of hot water, if using Basmati rice, or follow instructions on the packet, and cook until done.

indian bread or rotis

The indigenous breads of India are unleavened breads known as roti (similar to the French word for "roast", *rotie*), made from ground wholewheat (*aata*), millet (*bajra*), or sorghum (*jowar*). The latter two are eaten in rural Western and Central India, while wheat is the main cereal in Northern India and most of urban India, except in coastal Southern and all of Eastern India where rice is the main cereal. The Muslim-influenced breads of India are leavened, like the naans, Khamiri rotis and various other kinds of roti breads of Mumbai.

The dough is made with the ground cereal and tepid water (water described as tepid in the tropics would be slightly warm in the temperature zone). Some people add a little ghee or oil to the dough because it makes the roti softer. Some rotis served in restaurants, such as the *roomali* roti (thin and large like a handkerchief), have eggs mixed in the dough.

Housewives in India still largely buy their grain whole and send it either fortnightly or monthly to a small shop in the neighbourhood for custom-grinding. They like to make sure they get the wheat without any adulteration. In the last few years, whole ground wheat flour in packets has made its appearance at grocers and is gaining acceptance, though there is no national popular brand. The dough for most rotis is fairly standard, as follows:

dough mixture

1 cup wholemeal flour
1/3 cup warm water
2 teaspoons ghee or oil

Mix the water and flour together to make a dough, by hand or in a food-processor. Then add the ghee or oil and knead it by hand for at least 5, preferably 8 minutes, as this process will make the dough slightly elastic, and the rotis will have a softer texture.

For best results, cover with a damp cloth and leave for 1 hour. With this mixture you can make 12 light chapatis or pooris, or 6 parathas. These should be enough for 3 persons.

chapati

You need a griddle to make chapatis. In India, the chapati griddle is made of cast iron, is slightly concave and is known as a *tawa*. Since it is used every day it does not have a chance to rust. Sprinkle a little dry flour onto a rolling board. Place the ball of dough on this and flatten. Sprinkle a little flour on top. Roll out gently to a thin pancake about 6-in in diameter. Sprinkle over a tiny amount of flour, if necessary, to facilitate rolling, but not too much or the chapatis will turn out dry. Put onto a hot griddle over a high heat. When brown spots appear, turn

Opposite, clockwise from top: naan, paratha, poori, chapati

over, and let it cook completely, particularly at the sides, pressing down with a spoon if necessary. Turn it over once more so that the first side, which had been just slightly cooked, gets completely done.

This is the procedure for chapatis to be made just before the meal. Wrap them in foil or in a vacuum box (as they are now kept in India) to keep them fresh before serving. If you want to make them several hours before the meal, brush them on both sides with a little oil when on the griddle, fold in half, and wrap the whole lot in foil. Then warm in an oven just before serving.

phulka

Some people prefer chapatis puffed up. For this you need an open flame beside the hot griddle.

Put the chapati on the griddle until brown spots appear, lift with a pair of tongs, and hold over an open flame. When cooked, turn over, and it will have puffed up. Dab with a little oil, ghee, or butter after removing from the heat. You can store the phulkas one on top of the other on a plate. These have to be eaten soon after making.

pooris

Pooris are eaten for breakfast in Northern India along with a potato preparation. They are also eaten by Gujaratis as part of the thali, and quite commonly in Bengal.

Divide the chapati dough into 12 balls and roll each out into a 5-in pancake, using a little wheat flour to do so. In a deep skillet, heat sufficient oil over a very high heat to cover the top surface of the poori immediately, otherwise they will not puff up, and deep-fry the poori individually, turning it over in the oil.

parathas

The paratha is an enriched chapati. You can season the dough with finely chopped mint leaves and a little salt and paprika if you wish.

Divide the chapati dough into 6 pieces. Using a little flour, roll out each piece to an oval about 8-in long. Then draw in the sides together with your fingers to form a figure of 8, and fold to make a 4-in double-layered pancake. Roll out again to about 7-in diameter.

Put a little ghee or oil on a hot griddle and put on the paratha to cook. When one side is done, brush with a little ghee and turn it over. Remove when done. Stack the parathas one on top of another, and if not serving immediately, wrap in foil. Reheat in an oven when serving.

Parathas can be stuffed with vegetables. The most popular stuffings are boiled and spiced potato or grated and spiced radish. Spices used are a little red chile, cumin powder, a pinch of dried mango powder, and salt.

side vegetables

Although a curry is not a "must" in an Indian meal, a vegetable dish is, both at lunch and dinner. In India a meal often consists of a vegetable dish or two, a lentil dal, a yogurt dish like a raita, and rotis and/or rice. So the dishes mentioned in this section can be considered as part of such a meal, or as a side dish to a curry. I have explained here only a few of the popular Indian vegetable dishes. They are actually quite simple to prepare.

spinach with curd cheese (palak paneer)

Serves 2

$^3/_4$ pint milk
$^1/_2$ cup live yogurt
salt
2 teaspoons lime or lemon juice
9oz fresh spinach or 1 small packet
   frozen spinach
2 green chiles, chopped

$^1/_2$ teaspoon chopped fresh ginger
2 tablespoons oil
a pinch of fenugreek seeds
1 onion, chopped
1 clove garlic, chopped
$^1/_4$ teaspoon cumin seeds
2 tomatoes, puréed

1 To make curd cheese, bring the milk just to boiling point, then add the live yogurt with a pinch of salt and the lime or lemon juice. Continue boiling for 7–10 minutes. The milk will separate. Remove from the heat and allow to cool.

2 Place a large strainer over a bowl and pour in the milk to collect the solids in the strainer, allowing the whey to remain in the bowl below. Keep the milk solids in contact with the whey until required for cooking. When ready to use, press down the solids in the strainer with a potato masher or the back of a large spoon to squeeze the moisture out, or use a jelly bag or cheesecloth. You will get about 4oz curd cheese or paneer.

3 Cook the spinach with the chiles, ginger, a pinch of salt, and just a sprinkling of water if using fresh spinach. Cook uncovered so that the bright green color is retained. (Salt is also required for retaining the color.) When cool, purée in a blender.

4 In a skillet, heat the oil and fry the fenugreek seeds for 30 seconds, then add the onion and fry until lightly colored. Add the garlic and cumin, and after 30 seconds the tomatoes. Fry for about 5 minutes.

5 When the liquid from the tomatoes has evaporated, add the curd cheese and stir gently. Add the puréed spinach and cook for a couple of minutes. It is now ready to serve.

stir-fried french beans (beans porial)

Serves 4

9oz french beans
1/2 teaspoon whole white urad dal
1/4 cup grated coconut
3/4 teaspoon cumin seeds
1 1/2 tablespoons finely chopped onion
10–12 curry leaves, finely chopped
salt
2 tablespoons oil or butter
1 green chile, finely chopped and de-seeded, if liked
1/3 teaspoon mustard seeds

1 De-string and top and tail the beans. Chop into 1/2-in pieces.

2 Soak the urad dal in 1/2 cup of water for 15 minutes. Drain and set aside.

3 Put the grated coconut into a bowl. Add the cumin seeds, onion, and curry leaves and mix well.

4 Boil the beans in 1 cup of water with 1/4 teaspoon of salt for 5 minutes, uncovered. The salt will help retain the bright green color. Drain.

5 Heat the oil or butter in a skillet and fry the chiles until pale green, then add the mustard seeds and after 20 seconds, add the urad dal grains. After 1 minute, add the coconut and onion and sauté, stirring continuously for 2 minutes. Add the beans, toss, and cook for a few minutes over a low heat until the beans are tender.

Opposite, anti-clockwise, from the top: cabbage with spices and tomato, stuffed baby eggplants, cabbage with mustard seeds, peas and carrots with cumin

cauliflower with shredded ginger (punjabi gobi)

Cauliflower is believed to be heavy to digest and to cause wind, particularly if water is added during cooking. So in Northern India especially, cauliflower is cooked without adding any liquid. Ginger and cumin aid digestion and help to avoid flatulence. This is a very popular way of cooking cauliflower, and very tasty too.

Serves 4

1lb 2oz cauliflower
$3/4$ teaspoon cumin seeds
3 tablespoons oil
1–2 tablespoons grated fresh ginger
a pinch of red chile powder
$1/4$ teaspoon cumin powder
salt
a pinch of garam masala

1 Cut the cauliflower into florets. Pound the cumin seeds.

2 Heat the oil in a wok and fry the ginger. After 30 seconds, add the pounded cumin seeds and the chile and cumin powders. Then add $1/4$–$1/2$ teaspoon of salt, stir, and add the cauliflower.

3 Sprinkle with the garam masala powder and stir well. Cover with a lid and cook over a low heat until the cauliflower is as tender as you like it. It is now ready to serve.

cabbage with spices and tomato

Serves 4

1lb cabbage
2 medium onions
1/2 x 1/4-in piece of fresh ginger
1 green chile
2 medium tomatoes

3 tablespoons oil
1/8 teaspoon turmeric powder
1 teaspoon coriander powder
1/2 teaspoon red chile powder
salt

1 Grate or slice the cabbage very finely and separate into shreds. Chop the onions, ginger, and chile very finely. Chop the tomatoes.

2 Heat the oil in a wok. Add the onion, ginger, and chile and sauté until the onion is browned. This takes about 25 minutes.

3 Add the cabbage. Sprinkle in the turmeric, coriander, and red chile powders. Mix well. Cover with a lid and cook for 10 minutes, then add the tomatoes and salt to taste and cook until done.

stuffed baby eggplants (masala baingan)

Serves 2–3

1 teaspoon coriander powder
1/4 teaspoon cumin powder
1/4 teaspoon turmeric powder
1/4 teaspoon red chile powder
1/4 teaspoon dried mango powder

1/8 teaspoon salt
1 teaspoon sugar
9oz baby eggplants
3 tablespoons oil

1 Mix together all the spices, salt, and sugar. Make cross-slits on top of the eggplants, about 1-in deep. Stuff the spice mixture into the slits.

2 Heat the oil in a non-stick or thick-bottomed skillet with a lid, and add the stuffed eggplants. Cover and cook over a low heat, turning from time to time, for about 15 minutes, until tender.

cabbage with mustard seeds

Serves 2

14oz cabbage, finely shredded
salt
4 tablespoons oil
¹/₄ teaspoon mustard seeds

1 green chile, chopped
¹/₄-in square piece of fresh ginger, chopped
about 10 curry leaves
¹/₃ teaspoon sugar

1 Soak the cabbage in water with a little salt for 15 minutes, then drain.

2 Heat the oil in a deep skillet and add the mustard seeds. When they pop, add the chile, ginger, and curry leaves and sauté for 1 minute. Add the cabbage, salt to taste, and sugar. Sauté, mixing all the ingredients well. Cook over a low heat, uncovered, until it reaches your preferred consistency.

okra with chopped onions (bhindi pyaz)

Serves 2

9oz okra (bhindi)
salt
2 tablespoons oil
2 medium onions, chopped
1–2 green chiles
³/₄ teaspoon cumin seeds, crushed

1 Wash the okra and soak in a bowl of water with a pinch of salt for 5 minutes. With a sharp knife, trim away the stem just above the ridge. Chop the okra into ³/₄-in pieces.

2 Heat the oil in a large, non-stick skillet. Sauté the onions until browned. Add the chiles and fry until pale green, then add the cumin seeds and fry for 30 seconds.

3 Add the okra and salt. Stir well. Cook over a low heat, uncovered. Stir from time to time to prevent the okra sticking to the pan. Cook until done.

peas and carrots with cumin (gajar mutter)

Serves 2

3 tablespoons oil
2 medium onions, finely chopped
1 green chile, finely chopped
1 clove garlic, finely chopped
1/2-in square piece of fresh ginger, finely chopped
1/4 teaspoon coriander powder
1 teaspoon cumin powder
1/4 teaspoon red chile powder
1/2 teaspoon cumin seeds
1 small tomato, chopped
1 cup peas, fresh or frozen (shelled weight)
3oz carrots, diced
salt

1 Heat the oil in a non-stick skillet over a low heat and sauté the onion until brown. This will take 20–25 minutes. Then add the green chile, garlic, and ginger. Sauté for 3 minutes.

2 Add the coriander, cumin, and red chile powders, and the cumin seeds, and sauté for 2 minutes. Add 3 tablespoons of water and stir well. Continue cooking the spices for 3 minutes.

3 Add the tomato and cook for a further 2–3 minutes. Then add the peas and carrots, salt to taste, and cover and cook until tender.

potatoes

Potatoes are a very popular vegetable throughout India. They are eaten by themselves or combined with other vegetables like cauliflower, cabbage, capsicum, french beans, and peas. For potatoes in a curry, see Creamy Potato Curry (*Malaidhar Aloo*) on page 162.

The following recipes are all for dry potato dishes to be eaten with any curry or lentil dish.

potatoes gujerati-style

1lb 2oz potatoes
1/2 teaspoon turmeric powder
salt
2 tablespoons oil
1/2 teaspoon mustard seeds
1/2 teaspoon washed white
  urad dal
16–20 curry leaves
1/2 teaspoon chile powder
1/4 teaspoon sugar

1 Boil the potatoes in their skins with the turmeric powder and 1 teaspoon of salt. When they are 90 per cent done, drain, cool, and peel. Cut into small pieces.

2 Heat the oil in a wok, add the mustard seeds and urad dal. After 10 seconds, add the curry leaves and chile powder. After 5 seconds, add a little water and cook for 3 minutes, then add the sugar and an additional seasoning of a little salt.

3 Toss the potatoes in this mixture and cook for a few minutes until they are done and heated through, and have absorbed some of the oil.

potatoes with fenugreek leaves (aloo methi) *punjab and sindh*

9oz potatoes, preferably new
3/4 cup fenugreek leaves
salt
3 tablespoons oil
2 cloves garlic, chopped
1 green chile, chopped
1/8 teaspoon turmeric powder
4 stalks of fresh dill, chopped
1 tablespoon chopped cilantro leaves

1 If not using new potatoes, peel and cut into bite-sized pieces. New potatoes can be left whole with the skins on.

2 Soak the fenugreek leaves in a bowl of water with a pinch of salt for 30 minutes. This will remove the slightly bitter taste. Then drain and chop.

3 Heat the oil in a large skillet or wok. Add the garlic and chile. After a few seconds, add the fenugreek leaves and fry for 1 minute.

4 Add the potatoes, turmeric powder, and salt to taste and stir-fry for 2 minutes, then add the dill and cilantro leaves.

5 Cover, reduce the heat to very low and leave to cook for 15 minutes, or until the potatoes are done. If necessary sprinkle with just a little water.

potatoes with peanuts

1lb potatoes
a pinch of turmeric powder
salt
2oz peanuts
4 tablespoons ghee or oil
1 teaspoon cumin seeds
1/4 teaspoon asafoetida (optional)
1–2 green chiles, finely chopped
a few curry leaves

1 Boil the potatoes in their skins with the turmeric powder and salt to taste. When done, drain, plunge into cold water, and peel off the skins.

2 Pound the peanuts or grind coarsely. Heat the ghee or oil in a cooking pot. When really hot, add the cumin seeds and, when they pop, sprinkle in the asafoetida, if used, and the chiles and curry leaves. Add the potatoes and peanuts and a pinch of salt, and stir gently so that the potatoes are properly seasoned and thoroughly hot.

3 Cook for 2 minutes and allow to heat through, then remove and serve.

Clockwise, from the top: potatoes in yogurt, fried potatoes with mixed spices,
potatoes with fenugreek leaves, potatoes with peanuts, potatoes gujerati-style

fried potatoes with mixed spices (sukha aloo)

1lb 2oz potatoes
1/2 teaspoon turmeric powder
salt
1/3 cup oil
1/2 teaspoon coriander powder
1 teaspoon red chile powder
1/2 teaspoon garam masala
  powder
1/3 teaspoon dried mango
  powder (amchoor)

1 Boil the potatoes in their skins with the turmeric powder and salt to taste for 5 minutes. Drain and cool, then peel off the skins. Cut into large fat chips or smaller bite-sized pieces.

2 Put the oil into a wok (preferably non-stick) with the coriander and chile powders. Let these spices heat up with the oil over a very low heat. As soon as the oil is hot, add the potatoes and stir well. Cover with a lid and leave to cook for about 20 minutes. Stir from time to time.

3 When almost done, add the garam masala powder and toss a couple of times. When ready, sprinkle with the mango powder and toss just once, then serve.

potatoes in yogurt (dahiwalla aloo) *maharashtrian-style*

1lb 2oz potatoes
2 medium onions
2oz fresh coconut, grated
3–4 green chiles
2 cloves garlic
1 x 1/2-in piece of fresh ginger
1 1/2 teaspoons coriander powder
1 teaspoon cumin powder
1/2 teaspoon turmeric powder
1 teaspoon red chile powder
2 tablespoons plain yogurt
2 tablespoons oil
1/8 teaspoon mustard seeds
a few curry leaves or 1 tablespoon cilantro leaves
salt

1 Peel the potatoes and cut crossways into round slices about 1/2-in thick.

2 Purée the onions, coconut, green chiles, garlic, ginger, coriander, cumin, half the turmeric, and the red chile powder with 2 tablespoons of water in a blender or food-processor.

3 Whisk the yogurt well with a fork and set aside.

4 Boil the potatoes with the remaining turmeric powder and salt to taste (about 1 teaspoon). When the potatoes are 75 per cent done, drain and cool.

5 Heat the oil in a wok and add the mustard seeds. When they pop, add the curry or cilantro leaves, followed by the puréed spices. Fry for 8–10 minutes, stirring from time to time.

6 Add the whisked yogurt and mix well. Now add 1/2 cup of water, taste, and season with salt. Add the sliced potatoes and cook over a low heat until done (about 15 minutes).

lentils (dals)

Dal with rice is the national dish of India. It is also eaten with rotis by the highest and lowest, from north India to the south and east to west. All the amino acids absent from rice are found in dal, which makes the combination the perfect vegetarian protein dish. It is also easy to digest.

Different dals are popular in different parts of India. In the Punjab and Delhi, the most popular is black urad dal, but it is cooked with an immense amount of butter and ghee, so I am omitting it from this book. Also, it is not ideal for eating with a curry meal. In the east, the gram dal is popular: in fact it is known as Bengal gram (chana dal). In the Uttar Pradesh, north and west India moong dal is liked. It is easy to digest and as such is given to convalescents. In Uttar Pradesh, the state in India through which most of the River Ganges runs and from where the best dal dishes come, the masoor dal is also popular and prepared very well. In the south, the most commonly eaten dal is the toor dal, also known as arhar dal. It is used for making sambhar, a dish made of ground spices, eaten daily.

These dals come in various forms: whole or split, in the case of moong with the skin on or off, washed or unwashed, or oiled or un-oiled. Cooked dals can be kept in the refrigerator for 2 days.

moong dal *uttar pradesh-style*

7oz yellow moong dal
2 large tomatoes, chopped
2 green chiles, chopped
1-in square piece of fresh ginger, chopped
3 plump cloves garlic, chopped

¹/₄ teaspoon turmeric powder
salt
1 tablespoon chopped cilantro leaves
about 8 curry leaves
1 tablespoon butter or oil

1 Wash the dal well. Soak for 15 minutes.

2 Bring 5 cups of water to a boil in a cooking pot. Add the dal with the tomatoes, chiles, ginger, two-thirds of the garlic, the cloves, and the turmeric powder. Return to a boil, then add salt to taste. Cook for 30 minutes. Remove from the heat and whisk gently with an egg beater, until the grains are completely mashed. Add the cilantro and curry leaves and cook for 5 minutes.

3 Heat the butter or oil in a ladle, add the remaining garlic and fry until golden. Pour into the dal, which is now ready to serve. The consistency should be like a creamy soup.

Clockwise, from the top right: dal of bengal gram, dry moong dal,
moong dal uttar pradesh-style, masoor dal uttar pradesh-style

masoor dal *uttar pradesh-style*

9oz pink masoor dal	$1/2$-in square of fresh ginger, chopped
5 cloves garlic	2–3 green chiles, chopped
1 teaspoon tamarind pulp (optional)	1 teaspoon coriander powder
salt	$1/2$ teaspoon cumin powder
7oz red pumpkin, chopped	1 teaspoon red chile powder
1 medium onion, chopped	2 teaspoons lime juice
3 small tomatoes, chopped	1 tablespoon oil or butter

1 Wash the dal well and soak for 30 minutes.

2 Chop 3 garlic cloves and keep separate from the other 2, which should also be chopped.

3 Soak the tamarind, if used, in $1/2$ cup of warm water for 30 minutes.

4 Bring 7 cups of water to a boil in a cooking pot. Add the dal, return to a boil, and add 1 teaspoon of salt. Also add the pumpkin, onion, tomatoes, 3 garlic cloves, ginger, green chiles, and the coriander, cumin, and red chile powders. Cook for 30 minutes over a moderate heat.

5 Add the tamarind water (if used) and lime juice through a strainer. Boil for 2 minutes, then remove from the heat and whisk gently with an egg beater, until the grains are completely mashed.

6 When ready to serve, heat the oil or butter in a ladle and fry the remaining chopped garlic for 1 minute. Add to the dal. The consistency should be like a soft porridge.

dal of bengal gram chana dal *(in bengal, chular dal)*

9oz Bengal gram (chana dal)
1 tablespoon oil or ghee
1 tablespoon raisins, plus extra to garnish
salt
2 cloves garlic, chopped
1/2-in piece of fresh ginger, chopped
2 green chiles, chopped
1 cinnamon or bay leaf

1/2 teaspoon cumin seeds
3/4 teaspoon red chile powder
1/2 teaspoon turmeric powder
1 tomato, chopped
1/2 teaspoon sugar (optional)
a pinch of asafoetida
1 tablespoon chopped cilantro leaves

1 Wash the dal well. Soak for 15–20 minutes.

2 Put half the oil or ghee into a ladle, hold over heat, add the raisins, and fry for 1 minute. Set aside on kitchen paper. Cook the dal in 2 1/2 cups of water for 20 minutes until soft. Add 1 teaspoon of salt. Remove from the heat and leave the dal in the pot.

3 Put the remaining oil or ghee into a small skillet and sauté the garlic, ginger, green chiles, and cinnamon or bay leaf. After 2 minutes, add the cumin, red chile, and turmeric powders and stir well. Add the tomato and continue to stir for a further 2 minutes.

4 Add this mixture to the dal with the sugar, if used, and the fried raisins and asafoetida. Bring to a boil and cook until the grains are very soft, though they should remain semi-separate. When serving, reheat the dal and garnish with fresh cilantro leaves and chopped raisins.

In Bengal, sugar is added. In Bangladesh no sugar is added to this dish. The asafoetida is supposed to aid digestion and prevent flatulence as Bengal gram is heavy to digest.

dry moong dal churi dal, sindhi-style

Churi means "separate" in Sindhi, so this dal has a consistency similar to rice, where the dal grains are separate and dry when cooked.

5oz yellow moong dal
salt
a pinch of turmeric powder
_$^1/_4$ teaspoon coriander powder_
_$^1/_4$ teaspoon cumin powder_
_$^1/_4$ teaspoon red chile powder_
_$^1/_4$ teaspoon dry mango powder (amchoor)_
_$^1/_4$ teaspoon butter or oil_

1 In a small cooking pot, bring 1 cup of water to a boil and add the dal. Return to a boil, then add salt to taste. Cook until all the water is absorbed, then turn the heat to very low, put a griddle pan over the heat, and place the pot with the dal on it. This gives an even, mild heat, which prevents the dal from sticking to the bottom of the pot. All the remaining moisture will become absorbed in about 20 minutes.

2 When ready to serve, put the hot dal in a serving bowl. Sprinkle evenly with the spice powders, adding them one by one. Then heat the butter or oil in a ladle, and when very hot pour over the spices. Cover the bowl with a lid for a few seconds, then remove and serve. The consistency should be that of soft rice.

yogurt (raitas)

Raitas are simple to make. Essentially the yogurt has to be whipped or whisked. You can make it with plain or reduced-fat yogurt. If making it with plain yogurt, then add a little water to thin it.

Season with salt, pepper, and cumin powder. Then add a little sugar if desired, especially if the yogurt is slightly sour. This is the basic raita recipe. Then you can add chopped cilantro leaves if you wish, and sprinkle with red chile powder or paprika. This is done in the serving bowl because it looks attractive as well as giving a slightly pungent taste.

A favorite addition to raitas, especially when making *chaat* (spicy street food), is to add a few teaspoons of red or tamarind chutney on the top, which gives it a nice tang. The recipe for a red chutney which goes well with raita is given on page 200.

You can also add other ingredients of your choice. Chopped cucumber, potato, tomato, or onion are the most popular ingredients in everyday versions. Other commonly used ingredients in raita are boiled white pumpkin, boiled baby eggplants, blanched strips of spinach, which can also be combined with raisins or dates, and *bhoondi*—tiny balls of fried besan or gram flour. Sindhis and Gujaratis also add *sev,* a small string-like snack made from gram flour, which is part of Bombay Mix. So mix and match as you prefer.

Incidentally, raitas are very cooling, so Indians avoid them in the evenings in winter.

cucumber raita

1 cup plain yogurt
$^1/_2$ cup or more cucumber, peeled and finely chopped
salt and pepper
$^1/_8$ teaspoon cumin powder
$^1/_2$ teaspoon sugar
a pinch of paprika powder
1 teaspoon finely chopped cilantro leaves

Whisk the yogurt. Add a little water if desired. Add the cucumber, salt, pepper, cumin powder, and sugar. Mix well. Put into a serving bowl and garnish with paprika and cilantro leaves.

potato raita

1 large potato
salt and pepper
1 1/2 cups plain yogurt
1/8 teaspoon cumin powder and a pinch of paprika powder
1 teaspoon chopped cilantro leaves

Boil the potato in its skin with a little salt until cooked. When cool, peel and cut into small cubes. Whisk the yogurt. Add a little water if desired. Add salt and pepper to taste and the cumin, and mix well. Add the potatoes and stir gently. Put into a serving bowl. Garnish with paprika and cilantro leaves.

spinach raita

15 leaves spinach, well washed
1 cup yogurt
salt and pepper and 1/8 teaspoon cumin powder
12–15 seedless raisins or 3 dates (optional)
a pinch of paprika powder

Cut the spinach into fine strips. Boil with a pinch of salt for 3–4 minutes in 1 cup of water, then drain. Whisk the yogurt. Season with salt and pepper to taste and add the cumin. Add the spinach and raisins or dates, cut into thin strips if liked. Pour into a serving bowl and sprinkle with paprika.

tomato raita

1 cup yogurt
salt and pepper, and 1/8 teaspoon cumin powder
1 large tomato, finely chopped
1/8 onion, finely chopped
1 teaspoon cilantro leaves

Whisk the yogurt, adding a little water if desired. Season with salt and pepper to taste and add the cumin. Combine with the tomato and onion and pour into a serving bowl. Garnish with cilantro leaves.

Clockwise, from top right: potato raita, spinach raita, tomato raita,
and cucumber raita

papadams

Papadams (*papads* in India) are eaten with every dal and rice meal, and often with curry too. In certain parts of India, such as the south, they are an essential feature, in others optional.

Papadams are made from either lentils (of various kinds) or from a combination of lentil and rice flour. The rice flour papadams are from south India, and need to be fried. The lentil ones are from Northern India and can be toasted or fried. The lentil ones are seasoned with either black pepper, or garlic and chile, or herbs and spices. Nowadays tiny papadams are produced for frying, which can be served with meals or as cocktail snacks. They are colloquially known as disco papads in Mumbai. There, anything new and likable is given the prefix disco!

In north India it is believed that papads act as fat absorbers in the body. Sindhis always follow a meal with toasted papads and only then drink water as they believe that drinking water without eating a papad may lead to a cough. To toast a lentil papad, heat a griddle or crêpe pan until very hot, then toast the papad on both sides, pressing down the edges to ensure that they do not remain raw. Toasted papads can be kept for a couple of hours. Alternatively you can hold papads directly over an open gas flame. Sometimes a little oil or butter is put on the griddle pan and when hot, the papad is roasted on it. Fried papads cannot be kept for long as they will go soggy.

For parties and special occasions, make in this way with a little butter or oil, and garnish with a few finely chopped cilantro leaves, red chile or paprika, and finely chopped desiccated coconut: tasty and attractive.

You can cook them an hour or so ahead and keep on the dining table.

red chile papad

plain papad

mini papads

south india papad

black pepper papad

chutneys

The word chutney comes from the word *chaat-na*—to lick! So chutney is something that is finger-licking good. It can be made by grinding fresh ingredients or by cooking some ingredients. Chutneys are always vegetarian, and have a sour tang: Indians like sour things and also believe that eating something sour at every meal is good for health.

Tomato chutney is made all over India. Purely herb chutneys are eaten in west and north India. Coconut chutneys are popular in Southern India and herb and coconut chutneys in Western India. Mint and yogurt is eaten in the Punjab and Delhi. Walnut chutney is eaten in Kashmir and groundnut chutney in Andhra Pradesh. Chutney keeps, covered in a fridge, for 2 days; thereafter the flavor deteriorates fast.

green chutney with coconut

³/₄ cup cilantro leaves
1 tablespoon mint leaves
³/₄ cup grated fresh coconut
2 green chiles
1 clove garlic

1 teaspoon chopped fresh ginger
¹/₂ teaspoon salt
¹/₃ teaspoon cumin powder
1 teaspoon caster sugar
2 teaspoons lime juice

Grind together all the ingredients except the lime juice in a blender, without adding any water. When the mixture is ground to a smooth paste, remove and put into a small serving bowl. Add the lime juice and mix well with a teaspoon. Serve with all coconut-based curries and *dhansak*.

green chutney

1 cup mint leaves
1 cup cilantro leaves
1 or 2 green chiles, chopped
¹/₂ small onion, chopped

¹/₄ teaspoon cumin powder
¹/₄ teaspoon salt
1 teaspoon sugar
2 teaspoons lime or lemon juice

Purée all the ingredients except the lime or lemon juice. Then add the juice and stir well.

red chutney

1 cup grated fresh coconut
1 small onion, chopped
2 teaspoons chopped cilantro leaves
3/4-in piece of fresh ginger, chopped
1 1/2 teaspoons red chile powder
1/2 teaspoon cumin powder

2 cloves garlic
1 teaspoon sugar
3 tablespoons tomato ketchup
6 dates, stoned
2 teaspoons lime juice
1/2 teaspoon salt

Put all the ingredients into a blender and grind to a paste.

groundnut chutney

4oz peanuts
1 tablespoon tamarind pulp
2 green chiles
1 teaspoon salt
10 curry leaves
1 onion

1 teaspoon oil
1/2 teaspoon cumin seeds
1/2 teaspoon fenugreek seeds
1/2 teaspoon urad dal
2 tablespoons grated fresh coconut

1 Dry-roast the peanuts (even if they have skins) for about 15 minutes in a skillet, with no oil. When the peanuts begin to burn, remove from the heat. Leave to cool, then remove any skins.

2 Soak the tamarind for 10 minutes in 1/4 cup of water. Put all the ingredients into a food-processor or blender, and grind to a paste.

Clockwise, from top right: red chutney, green chutney, green chutney with coconut

cachumbers or relishes

Cachumber is to an Indian meal what salsa is to a Mexican one. It provides raw vegetables with a tangy touch. The classic cachumber is made with raw onions, and there are many variations of this. It is finely chopped with tomato, cilantro leaves (and green chile for those who like it), and seasoned with lime juice and salt. Variations are finely sliced onions with salt, chile powder, and lime juice.

Indians generally like to eat raw onion both for taste and for health. Onions contains sulphur, and they believe a little bit in its raw form is good. They don't worry too much about its effect on the breath; they would rinse their mouth after a meal, and chew a betel leaf, clove, or green cardamom as a breath freshener. Onions are a stimulant of passions, so Brahmin families do not eat them either cooked or raw.

In Western India, in Maharashtra and along the west coast, cachumbers are particularly popular and varied, and are known as *koshumbir*. They are made with all kinds of vegetables. Recipes for cabbage and carrots are given below. They are so tasty that they can be served as a salad or side vegetable. These *koshumbir* recipes have been given by Anju Sirur.

classic onion and tomato cachumber

1 medium onion
1 medium tomato
1/4 green capsicum

2 teaspoons cilantro leaves
lime juice
salt

Finely chop the onion, tomato, capsicum, and cilantro leaves. Add lime juice and a pinch of salt to taste. Mix well.

sliced onion cachumber

1 onion
1/8 teaspoon paprika

lime juice to taste
a pinch of salt

Slice the onion very finely. Season with paprika, lime juice, and salt.

Clockwise from top right: carrot koshumbir, sliced onion cachumber,
classic onion and tomato cachumber, and cabbage koshumbir

cabbage koshumbir

$^1/_4$ cabbage
$^1/_4$ fresh coconut or 2oz
  desiccated coconut
$^1/_2$ mild green chile (optional)
$^1/_4$ capsicum
juice of 1 lime

$^1/_2$ teaspoon superfine sugar
salt
2 tablespoons ghee or oil
a pinch of mustard seeds
8–10 curry leaves

1 Grate the cabbage finely. Finely grate the fresh coconut, if using. Very finely chop the lower half of the green chile, if using. Chop the capsicum and reserve for garnishing.

2 Make a dressing with the lime juice, sugar, and a pinch of salt. Mix the chopped cabbage, coconut, and green chile and pour over the dressing evenly. Mix well.

3 In a ladle, heat the ghee or oil, add the mustard seeds and when they pop, add the curry leaves. Remove from the heat after 30 seconds and mix with the cabbage. Transfer to a serving dish and garnish with chopped capsicum.

carrot koshumbir

1lb carrots
$^2/_3$ cup desiccated fresh coconut
$^1/_2$ cup roasted peanuts
juice of 1 lime
$^1/_2$ teaspoon superfine sugar

$^1/_2$ teaspoon salt
2 mild green chiles (optional)
2 tablespoons oil
$^1/_4$ teaspoon cumin seeds

1 Grate the carrots and fresh coconut, if used, and mix together. Grind the peanuts in a coffee grinder to a very coarse consistency. Make a dressing with the lime juice, sugar, and salt. Mix with the carrots and coconut.

2 Make a half-slit in the chiles, if used. Heat the oil in a ladle, add the cumin seeds and after 10 seconds, add the chiles, if used. After another 10 seconds, pour the mixture over the carrots. Mix well, reserving the chiles as a garnish.

desserts

mango mousse

Serves 6

1³/₄lb canned Alphanso mango pulp
1 cup heavy cream

1 tablespoon powdered gelatin
2 egg whites
2 teaspoons superfine sugar
juice of 1 lime

1 Put the mango pulp into a bowl. Beat with an electric whisk.

2 In a separate bowl, whisk the cream until it is lightly whipped. Dissolve the gelatin in a little hot water.

3 Whisk the egg white with an electric whisk until they form soft peaks. Mix the dissolved gelatin and sugar into the egg white. Add the lime juice. Fold in the whisked cream and mango. Mix well, lightly but thoroughly. Put into a large serving bowl or individual bowls and leave to set in the refrigerator for at least 3 hours.

shrikand (flavored hung yogurt)

This is a wonderful sweet or sour yogurt dessert and is so easy to make. It is served on auspicious occasions in Maharashtra.

Serves 3

1³/₄ pints yogurt
4 teaspoons milk
¹/₂ teaspoon or less saffron

2–3 tablespoons superfine sugar (to taste, depending on the acidity of the yogurt)
¹/₄ teaspoon cardamom powder
1 tablespoon ground almonds (optional)
a few slivered almonds

1 Hang the yogurt in a piece of cheesecloth over a bowl for 3 hours and drain off the whey.

2 Put the milk and saffron into a bowl and mix vigorously with a spoon, so that the flavor of the saffron blends with the milk and it becomes deep gold in color.

3 When the yogurt is fully drained, combine with the saffron milk and add the sugar. Mix well to get a smooth consistency using a whisk or blender. It should have the consistency of whipped cream. Then mix in the cardamom powder and ground almonds, if used.

4 Put into a large serving bowl or individual bowls, garnish with slivered almonds, and leave to set in the refrigerator for 1 hour.

kulfi (indian ice cream)

A favorite Indian dessert, kulfi (opposite) is an ice cream traditionally made by reducing the milk by boiling it for a very long time. However, it is also easy to make with evaporated milk. Traditional kulfi moulds are made of aluminum but are now available in plastic. Alternatively you can make the ice cream in an ice-cube tray.

4 tablespoons sugar
3 cardamoms
2 x 1lb cans evaporated milk
about 12 strands of saffron
3 tablespoons heavy cream
2 leaves of silver leaf, to decorate (optional)

1 Add the sugar and cardamoms to the milk in a heavy-based saucepan, and cook over a low heat for 10 minutes, stirring and scraping the sides and bottom of the pan continuously. Remove from the heat. Remove the cardamoms and add the saffron. Mix well and leave to cool. Then stir in the cream.

2 Fill the kulfi moulds or pour the mixture into ice-cube trays. Freeze for 4–5 hours. Frozen kulfi keeps in the freezer like ice cream.

3 To remove from the moulds, dip each into hot water and press out the kulfi. Decorate with silver leaf, especially for festive occasions.

wholewheat halva (atte ka sera)

This dessert is relatively low in cholesterol (use a polyunsaturated oil), economical to make, and can be made in bulk and stored in a freezer. Children love it and it makes a good addition to brunch or high tea. In India, apart from being served as a dessert, it is also a winter breakfast dish. It is quite hard work to make as you have to stir frequently for at least 20 minutes, but the result is well worth the effort.

Serves 10

2 cups oil

3 cloves

5 cardamoms

2 cups wholewheat flour

1¹/₂ cups sugar

a little rosewater

¹/₂ cup raisins and chopped nuts

1 Heat the oil in a heavy-based cooking pot. Put the cloves and cardamoms in to fry and as they release aromas into the oil (this should take about 1 minute), add the flour. Stir well. Cook over a low heat for 15–20 minutes, stirring frequently until the mixture is nutty-brown.

2 Dissolve the sugar in 6 cups of hot water, add to the mixture, and cook for a further 7–10 minutes, stirring every now and then. It will become a sticky mixture. Remove from the heat and sprinkle in the rosewater. Serve hot, or re-heat when serving. Garnish with raisins and chopped nuts.

If kept at room temperature, excess oil will ooze out, which you can remove without affecting the taste of the dish.

shahi tukra (indian bread pudding)

Serves 4

4 slices white bread
1 cup ghee
3 cups canned evaporated milk
2¹/₂ tablespoons sugar
a few strands of saffron

a pinch of cardamom powder
2 teaspoons rosewater

To decorate
4 teaspoons pistachio nuts, pounded
2 leaves of silver leaf (optional)

1 Remove the crusts from the bread. Cut the slices in half diagonally. Heat half the ghee in a skillet and fry the slices of bread, one at a time, for 1¹/₂ minutes or until golden-brown. Remove and keep to one side on kitchen paper.

2 Make the sauce by cooking the evaporated milk and sugar in a heavy-based saucepan for 10 minutes over a low heat. Then remove from the heat and add the saffron, cardamom powder, and rosewater, mixing well.

3 To serve, place 2 slices of bread together and pour the sauce over them a short while before serving. Sprinkle with the pistachios and decorate with silver leaf.

apple halwa

Carrot halwa or *gajar ka halwa,* as it is called in India, is a popular dessert in Indian restaurants. Apple halwa can be made in the same way and has an interestingly sweet–tart taste. In restaurant kitchens, a form of milk cooked until all the water has evaporated—known as *mava* or *khoya*—is used. Condensed milk is a good substitute. This halwa is best made with Cox's apples.

Serves 2

1¹/₂lb apples, grated
2 teaspoons sugar
juice of ¹/₂ lemon
4 tablespoons ghee or clarified butter
1-in cinnamon stick
3 cloves

4 tablespoons condensed milk
1 tablespoon raisins
a knob of butter
2 tablespoons calvados (optional)
almond slivers, to decorate (optional)

1 As soon as the apples are grated, sprinkle with the sugar and lemon juice to prevent discoloration. Mix well.

2 Heat the ghee in a heavy-based saucepan, add the cinnamon and cloves and, after 30 seconds, the apples. Sauté for 8–10 minutes over a high heat. Add the condensed milk and raisins and sauté for a further 7–8 minutes, stirring continuously and scraping the bottom and sides of the pan.

3 Glaze with the butter. This dessert should be served hot. Heat the calvados, if using, for a few seconds in a small pan and pour into the halwa mixture. Garnish with the almonds, if using.

gulab jamuns

Serves 4

For the syrup

1lb sugar

1/4 lime, juice and zest

3 cardamoms

2 teaspoons rosewater or 2 drops keora water

1 cup baby milk powder

3 tablespoons self-rising flour

2 tablespoons cornstarch

1/4 teaspoon bicarbonate of soda

2 cups oil, for deep-frying

12 pistachio nuts

1 First make the syrup. Bring 2 1/2 cups of water to a boil. Add the sugar, lime juice and zest, and only the skins of the cardamoms (keep the seeds to one side). Boil on a low heat for 20 minutes. Leave to cool. Add the rosewater or *keora* water for aroma. Pour the syrup into a bowl at least 4-in deep.

2 Place the milk powder, flour, cornstarch, and bicarbonate of soda in a mixing bowl. Pound the cardamom seeds slightly and add. Mix well. Gradually, add a total of 3–4 tablespoons water, 1 tablespoon at a time, and make a dough. Try to get some air into the dough by teasing it with your hands. Knead for 6–7 minutes to a sticky texture. Finally put a little oil on your fingers and roll the dough in the bowl—it should now come away clean.

3 Heat the oil in a deep skillet, first on high and then, after 3 minutes, on low. Meanwhile, divide the dough into 12 portions and roll each portion well to make balls about 3/4-in in diameter, and stuff each with a pistachio.

4 Deep-fry the dough balls over the lowest possible heat for 5–7 minutes until they are dark brown. If they touch the hot metal of the pan they will stain and if the heat is high they will be uncooked inside. So stir constantly with a metal spoon so that they brown evenly. The stirring spoon will also prevent the oil from becoming too hot. The balls will expand in size.

5 As soon as you remove the *Gulab Jamuns* immerse them evenly in the cooled syrup and cover with a lid. They will be ready to eat after half an hour and should be eaten warm. They can be stored in the refrigerator for 5–6 days, and reheated when needed.

planning a meal

Friends in England often ask me how an Indian housewife plans her menu. While very much part of daily life, this is a complex matter, and a number of factors have to be considered. First, as anywhere else in the world, the season and availability of produce would be taken into account. Then, depending on the time of year, heating or cooling foods would be selected, and any special family requirements taken into account. According to the Ayurveda system, some foods increase certain tendencies. For example, it might be summer and cooling foods called for, while if someone in the family has a cough, onions and rice are to be avoided.

It is important to establish whether it is full moon or new moon, for many families would not cook non-vegetarian foods on such days. Then the family or personal deity that is worshipped has its particular day of the week. So many worshippers of Shiva, the god of creation, would either fast until sundown or eat only vegetarian food on a Monday. Similarly, Tuesday is the day of the monkey-god Hanuman, symbolising devotion and bravery. In Delhi, for example, restaurants experience a dip in their business on Tuesdays because many people are followers of Hanuman and, since they will not eat meat, avoid going out. The planets also have their corresponding days of the week. Some family members may have, say, Saturn malefic in their horoscope at the time, in which case the family astrologer would advise placating the planet by abstinence from particular foods—usually flesh of any kind—on Saturdays.

Once she has made her way through this maze of imponderables, the housewife gets down to the business of who is coming to dinner, what their special preferences are, and how hot or bland the dishes should be. Then she makes sure the colors of the various foods will balance, and works out how much time and help she has, and what she can afford.

In an Indian meal there is no such thing as a first course or appetizer. Appetites are automatically aroused by the wafting in of the various spicy aromas from the kitchen. All the food is placed on the table at once. The order in which it is eaten depends on the part of India in which the meal is taking place.

In a Westernized home, if only rice was being served, it would be put on the main plate, with the curry on the side or, if it had a thin gravy, in a small bowl like a compote or cereal bowl, with lentils and yogurt in even smaller bowls. The vegetables would also be put on the side of the main plate, as would the cachumber and chutney. The papadam may be on the side plate, along with the chapati if it is being served. This is not as complicated as it sounds, because the amounts of each item are small, and are replenished as required. Small portions of each item are eaten with the rice or chapati, or in combination, as desired.

An Indian family without domestic help would eat a simple meal with rice, curry, and a vegetable, with chapatis being made occasionally, perhaps only at weekends. They buy a lot of pitta bread, moisten it with a little water, heat it in the oven and serve it softened with a knob of butter.

suggested menus

menus with a mild curry

1 Lamb with apricots

Pulao rice (white rice flavored with
  whole spices)
Dry potatoes
Peas and carrots
Indian bread pudding (*Shahi Tukra*)

2 Lamb with plums

Saffron rice
Cauliflower with ginger
Potatoes with peanuts
Spinach raita
Tomato chutney
Kulfi ice cream

3 Chicken stew

White rice
French beans porial
Potatoes with curry leaves
Mango mousse

4 Fish molee

Dill rice
Green chutney with coconut
Onion and tomato cachumber
Fried papadams
Gulab Jamuns

5 Pineapple curry (vegetarian menu)

Creamy potato curry
Lemon or dill rice
Cabbage with mustard seeds
Potatoes with peanuts
Apple halwa

menus with medium spicy curries

6 Green chicken korma

Saffron rice
Masoor dal
Spinach with curd cheese
Potato raita with red chutney
Wholewheat halwa (in winter)
or Apple halwa (in summer)

7 Chicken dhansak

Pulao rice
Dry potatoes
Onion and tomato cachumber
Fried papadams
Green coconut chutney
Kulfi *or* ice cream *or* fresh fruit

8 Prawn patia

Yellow rice
Moong dal
Okra with tomatoes
Fried papadams
Indian bread pudding

9 Chickpea curry (vegetarian menu)

Yellow rice
Peas and carrots with cumin
Potatoes with yogurt
Green coconut chutney
Shrikand

menus with spicy curries

10 Lamb with turnips
or Parsee red chicken curry

White rice

Okra with tomatoes

Cucumber raita

Fruit salad

11   Andhra lamb curry or Chicken chettinad or Goa lamb vindaloo

Lemon rice

Potatoes with curry leaves

Spinach raita

Fried papadams

Tomato cachumber

Kulfi or ice cream or sorbet

12   Goa fish curry

Boiled rice

Potato raita with red chutney

Green chutney with coconut

Onion and tomato cachumber

Fried papadams

Mango mousse

menu where some guests are vegetarian and others not

13   Chicken curry with coconut Manglorean-style or Cauliflower and potato curry (using same spice mix)

White rice

Stuffed eggplant

Tomato raita

Green chutney with coconut

Fried papadams

Fruity ice cream or sorbet or Shrikand

a spicy vegetarian menu

14 Mixed vegetable curry

Lemon rice

Cucumber raita

Carrot cachumber

Fried papadams

Groundnut chutney

Shrikand

menu with medium spicy dryish curry—to be served with Indian breads

15 Lamb in pickling spices *or* Chicken pistachio korma *or* Butter chicken
Paratha *or* pitta bread (moistened, then heated in oven and served with knobs of butter)
Cauliflower with ginger
Potato raita
Onions and paprika cachumber (optional)
Tomato chutney
Fruit salad *or* Apple halwa

curry served with bread (for a meal, brunch or high tea)

16 Lamb slow-cooked in onions and yogurt
Sliced bread
Onions with paprika
Quarters of lime
Raita of your choice
Fresh fruit

a typical buffet menu

17 Meat curry with cumin-flavored potatoes
Malabar shrimp curry
Yellow rice
Chickpeas
French beans porial
Cucumber raita
Garnished papadams
   (using quarters of papads)
Tomato chutney
Mango mousse

what to drink with indian food

Drinking with food is not part of the middle-class Indian lifestyle. The most preferred alcoholic drink in India is scotch—for those who can afford it—failing which, Indian whisky. Beer, rum (largely in the armed services), vodka, and gin are also made in India and consumed by the upper middle classes, who now number over 30 million (the middle class itself is said to exceed 100 million).

But all drinking is done before dinner, accompanied by freshly made snacks, kebabs, and papadams. A minority of women drink, and they tend to prefer gin, vodka and, in recent years, Indian wine and champagne. A few wineries have set up in India and the quality of wine is improving. Red and white are produced, though the white is better. It is grown in different parts of the Deccan plateau, in Maharashtra, near Hyderabad, and near Bangalore. With 3 million Indians travelling overseas every year there is no doubt that India will develop a wine-drinking tradition. Dinner is eaten fairly late, between 8.30 and 9.30pm, and at dinner parties it would be considered inhospitable to serve dinner before 10.30pm (or even later), as it would imply that the host did not allow enough time for guests to drink their fill. At a party alcohol is considered more important than food, which in any case is always served buffet-style. But once eating begins, drinking comes to an end.

In everyday domestic situations, tepid water is sipped during a meal, and small quantities drunk thereafter. Cold water is generally avoided as it is believed to cause mucus in the stomach.

In Indian restaurants in the west it is popular to drink beer with Indian food, though in France the French enjoy wine with Indian food. It is all a matter of habit and custom. In the UK, lassi, a drink made of seasoned whisked yogurt diluted with water, is also popular with spicy Indian food, whereas in India, lassi is a breakfast drink consumed particularly in the summer.

index

acknowledgements

To my mother Sita who taught me good taste in childhood. My sister Namita who is today my best critic on taste. And the Taj Group of Hotels, which over 30 years gave me immense opportunities to travel through India and around the world, to see the best restaurants, to study many cuisines and to set up the first Szechwan restaurant in India—The Golden Dragon at the Taj in Bombay (1972), as well as the first Thai restaurant in India—Paradise Island in the West End Hotel in Bangalore (1988), which had its own Thai herb garden around it.

A debt is owed to all the chefs in India and overseas who shared their knowledge with me as well as the many others with whom I had the opportunity to work. And, of course, the many friends, home cooks, and wedding cooks who shared their treasure house of cooking secrets, so that people all over the world could enjoy the best Indian food.

Without Mike Shaw, my literary agent who agreed to represent me within a few moments of our meeting, and Kyle Cathie, the publisher of this book, who believed in it, in spite of the large amount of color photography involved, this book would not have seen its current form.

Photographic acknowledgements
Those taken by Peter Knab, styled by Diana Knab and with food preparation by Caroline Liddel, appear on pages 34, 37, 38, 39, 44, 48, 50, 51, 54, 55, 57, 58, 69, 71, 73, 79, 81, 83, 85, 89, 91, 93, 95, 99, 101, 103, 105, 111, 113, 117, 119, 121, 123, 127, 144, 147, 151, 196, 202

Those taken by Simon Smith, styled by Felicity Salter and with food preparation by Kathy Man, appear on pages 133, 135, 137, 139, 143, 148, 153, 155, 157, 159, 167, 170, 175, 178, 191, 198, 201, 207, 209

Those taken by Martin Brigdale, styled by Helen Trent and with food preparation by David Morgan, appear on pages 63, 64, 75, 77, 87, 97, 107, 109, 115, 125, 129, 131, 141, 161, 163, 165

Ashvin Mehta took the photographs on pages 4, 36; Ashvin Gatha that on page 53; Viren Desai those on pages 8, 21, 42 and Geoff Hayes those on pages 2–3, 11, 12, 15, 22, 25, 29, 46, 66–67, 169

An Hachette UK Company
www.hachette.co.uk

First published in Great Britain in 1994 by Kyle Books, an imprint of Kyle Cathie Ltd.
Carmelite House, 50 Victoria Embankment, London, EC47 0DZ
www.kylebooks.com

ISBN 978-0-857836-60-1

10 9 8 7 6 5 4 3 2 1

Text © Camellia Panjabi 1994, 2004
Design © Kyle Books 2004
Photographs © Peter Knab and Simon Smith 1994, Martin Brigdale 2004

Distributed in the US by Hachette Book Group,
1290 Avenue of the Americas, 4th and 5th Floors,
New York, NY 10104

Distributed in Canada by Canadian Manda Group,
664 Annette St., Toronto, Ontario, Canada M6S 2C8

Senior editor: Muna Reyal
Designer: Geoff Hayes
Recipe photography: Peter Knab, Simon Smith, Martin Brigdale; see also page 223
Food stylist for the recipe photography: Caroline Liddel, Kathy Man, David Morgan
Styling: Diane Knab, Felicity Salter, Helen Trent
Editorial assistant: Jennifer Wheatley
Production: Sha Huxtable and Alice Holloway

Printed and bound in China